contemporary kitchen style

contemporary
kitchen style

the essential handbook for an innovative design

by Mervyn Kaufman
and the editors of
Woman's Day Special Interest Publications

Copyright © 2009 Filipacchi
Publishing, a division of Hachette
Filipacchi Media U.S., Inc.

First published in 2009 in the
United States of America by
Filipacchi Publishing
1633 Broadway
New York, NY 10019

Woman's Day Special Interest
Publication is a registered trademark
of Hachette Filipacchi Media U.S., Inc.

Design: Patricia Fabricant
Editor: Lauren Kuczala
Production: Ed Barredo

ISBN-13: 978-1-933231-54-9

Library of Congress control number:
2008937591

Printed in China

contents

introduction

As editor of *Kitchens & Baths,* I see more than my fair share of kitchen designs; in the course of a week, maybe fifty projects come across my desk for review, each vying for a place in the pages of the magazine. Not to tip my hand, but frequently I'm drawn to spaces that are untraditional in nature.

Even ardent design fans may not know that "contemporary" and "modern" aren't necessarily synonymous. The latter, while celebrated in a recent renaissance, specifically refers to a school of design whose heyday was the 1920s. It's a disciplined look that emphasizes a regular geometry of pristine planes and blocky forms, all meticulously proportioned and minimal in detail. There's zero room for aesthetic error in modern design—you can't fall back on crown molding to hide a wavy ceiling or turned legs to fudge the scale of a central cooking island. When done without rigor, it's awful. But well-executed projects have an art and elegance to them that can be transcendental.

Contemporary design, on the other hand, is less bound by formula or historic precedent. This freedom poses its own challenges, however. A kitchen must work as well as it looks, so pragmatic planning becomes paramount in a contemporary space. Only after an efficient floor plan and lighting scheme have been developed can a bold—or subtle—approach to the kitchen's appearance be taken, and artistic boundaries broken.

In *Contemporary Kitchen Style,* author Mervyn Kaufman takes us inside many outstanding examples of both these forward-thinking styles created by leading architects and designers. Enjoy the journey—you're in the best of company.

—Leslie Plummer Clagett
Editor, *Kitchens & Baths*
Woman's Day Special Interest Publications

view minders

Kitchens were once inelegant spaces overlooking a garage or the neighbor's back fence. That concept changed with late 20th-century lifestyle shifts that pushed kitchens into the limelight and made them the heart of the home. Suddenly there was concern about access, light, and particularly views—of the patio, the garden, trees in a nearby forest. Homeowners began asking architects and designers to expand windows and make kitchens places not only to cook and live in but also in which to experience the great outdoors.

view with a room

when a terrific view meets a great kitchen design, that's residential nirvana. On the other hand, when kitchen walls obscure a spectacular view, as in the Toronto condominium of Jim and Aileen Reyes-Picknell, the impact can be dismal. "It was a disaster area," Jim declared, summing up the dark, tired kitchen that blocked the park panorama below his home.

Fortunately, Jim and kitchen designer Beverley Binns, of Binns Kitchen+Bath Design in Toronto, recognized that the space had great potential. Binns explained that her "goal was to take advantage of all the beautiful light and trees, and bring those visual elements into the space so they could be experienced when you first enter."

Hewing close to the original footprint of the 100-square-foot kitchen, Binns removed existing interior walls to integrate the windows—which wrap around the entire home—into the kitchen's design. This solution elicited childlike bliss from the homeowners. "We feel like we're living in a tree house!" said Aileen. "It's amazing to be putting away dishes and, at the same time, watching birds in the trees."

Crafted of rich cherry, the cabinets stand on stainless steel legs that suggest furniture placed in front of a window. Besides lending a freeform feel to the kitchen's overall design, this configuration allows heat to flow from a baseboard system, a holdover from the condo's former life as a commercial space. "The heat needed to circulate around the entire unit," Binns explained, "so we had to avoid covering that area."

The cabinets set an inviting tone that complements another focal point of the room: a stainless steel exhaust hood trimmed with glass. The hood hovers over three cooktop modules, including a barbecue that was near the top of Jim's kitchen wish list. An eating bar crafted from ¾-inch-thick solid glass sits on chrome posts and rests over a mostly quartz countertop. According to Jim, "It catches your eye right away, and it helps make the kitchen the social hub of the entire space."

For this couple, the kitchen is a place to create business as well as sustenance: They work out of their home, as both are management consultants for a company they founded. Now, they are able to plug their computers into outlets below the breakfast bar.

The couple avoided bulky appliances, streamlining the space by putting an oven and microwave side by side in the peninsula and paneling the refrigerator and dishwasher. A recessed shelf area displays barware, and a tambour-door cabinet set into a wall allows Jim and Aileen to hide small appliances instead of letting them clutter the countertops.

Jim and Aileen believe the room fuses style and function, and they have adopted its look throughout their home. "The kitchen looks so good and works hard at the same time," said Jim. "It's like paradise for us to live and work this way."

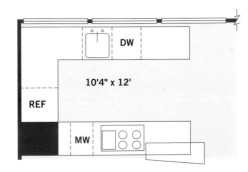

ABOVE: The kitchen's efficient U-shaped plan was given a new dimension when opened up to the windows that draw sunlight into the room.

OPPOSITE: The island-style exhaust hood features a shallow profile that barely interrupts views of lush greenery beyond the windows.

OPPOSITE: Elevating the breakfast bar on a stainless steel–supported glass slab above the counter not only echoes the steel legs of the base cabinets, but amplifies the floating effect that the designer was striving to achieve.

BOTTOM LEFT: Storage in this blind-corner cabinet is maximized by the installation of a movable shelf insert that puts the full depth of the cupboard to use.

BELOW: Everyday necessities for the table are kept close at hand but discreetly out of the way in a multiple-shelf wall niche finished to match the kitchen's cherry cabinetry.

reaching out

windows: Floor-to-ceiling windows wrap around the entire fourth-floor home and provide a breathtaking view. To embrace this element of the kitchen, designer Beverley Binns left all 19 feet of windows bare to maximize the impact of natural light pouring in.

lighting: "During the day, the space is flooded with sunlight," said Binns. But what about nighttime? The solid concrete ceiling precludes using recessed lighting, so Binns placed pendant lights near the vent hood and track lights over the sink. "At night, the pendants reflect off the glass and bring more light into the space," she added.

cabinets: Once the remodeling was complete, "there were no walls on which to hang traditional cabinets," said the designer. So she built a recessed wall to house the refrigerator and tambour cabinet and placed base cabinets on steel legs, allowing the feel of the kitchen to be more freeform.

country with a special twist

OPPOSITE: The granite-topped island kept getting bigger during the design process, as it acquired storage, dishwashing, and seating functions. Its remarkable mass eventually determined the dynamic U shape of the rest of the kitchen.

seeking something different, Brad and Deidre Wiener decided to go against the grain when they built their home in Campbell Hall, New York. Their tastes run to contemporary design; they happen to love clean lines, an uncluttered look, and one specific color—chocolate-brown—which was not particularly popular where their home was built.

Their kitchen became a major concern. "We were living in the country, and everyone we knew here had a country kitchen," Deidre recalled. "But we wanted something unique and special to us." Early in the planning stage, the couple decided that they would bring the same aesthetic to the kitchen that was evident in the rest of their home.

"The kitchen is very streamlined; each side is a mirror of the other," said Claudia Febres, a staff designer at Poggenpohl's New York City showroom who worked on the kitchen with Sherry Venokur, another New York–based designer. More fundamentally, however, the kitchen is also kosher.

A massive island was central to the design process. The Wieners wanted a sink and a dishwasher there so that, while she worked, Deidre could face the great room and her guests instead of having her back to them. The couple also wanted ample storage and comfortable seating for the whole family. As features accumulated, the island kept expanding. Its size helped the kitchen evolve into a large, symmetrical U shape. The legs of the U would become convenient, attractive sites for the dual appliances and double-the-usual storage spaces a kosher kitchen requires.

Designer Febres's biggest obstacle was the back wall of windows. Granted, they serve to bring the outdoors in and keep the kitchen naturally bright, but because they stretch from counter to ceiling, they don't leave much room for cabinets. To remedy this, Febres distributed storage space to each end of the U and also to the island.

With two each of dishwashers, ovens, warming drawers, and refrigerators, the Wieners wanted to make sure their kitchen did not wind up looking like an appliance showroom. In addition to paneling dishwasher and refrigerator fronts to integrate these appliances into the cabinets, Febres sought ways to break up the large space. "This wasn't a galley, where every inch counted," she pointed out. "We had the luxury of space and could make a statement with aesthetic elements."

Febres broke the space into defined workstations via a series of pilasters— brushed stainless steel columns—built into the cabinets. Stainless steel also complements the concrete countertops and granite-topped island, adding a sleek element. The vertical and horizontal lines of the elongated cabinet and drawer pulls, also finished in stainless steel, play off the pilasters.

Febres experimented with depths and heights, too. Beneath the exhaust hood, the cabinets between the pilasters are 30 inches deep. The cabinets she specified have a 9-inch toe-kick (4 inches is standard) so that people doing food prep at the counter can comfortably stand with their feet tucked under the cabinets. "It's ergonomic," said Febres. "It also heightens the impression that the cabinets are floating above the floor."

These custom touches certainly bring flair and individuality to the Wiener kitchen, giving the couple that unique space they wanted. But, ultimately, what they love most about their kitchen is that it is a warm, functional, hardworking space designed around their particular needs.

BELOW: As is evident in the plan, a clean, simple design will ensure that both the cooking and cleaning processes can take place smoothly and efficiently from station to station, with plenty of work and landing spaces.

BOTTOM: Countertops don't have to be 24 inches deep just because cabinets come that way. The Wieners learned that by installing their cabinets 6 inches away from the wall they could end up with spacious 30-inch-deep countertops.

BELOW: Counter-to-ceiling windows usher in glorious sunshine just as efficiently as they prohibit the installation of wall cabinets. That preempted storage space ended up along the walls of the U and in the very big island.

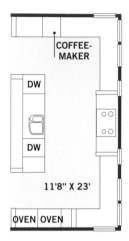

BELOW: In a kitchen with more than the usual number of appliances, custom panels help keep these workhorses from overwhelming the space. A microwave and coffeeemaker dominate the cabinet wall beside the refrigerator. Stainless steel pilasters also play a role in reducing the kitchen's mass by interrupting the flow of space.

strictly kosher

separate but equal Kosher kitchens must adhere to the practice of separating meat from dairy in the preparation, consumption, and storage of food. This means, for example, that the plates in one of these drawers (left) are only for meat and must not touch any dairy products, ever; those in the other drawer are for dairy and must never touch meat. Pots and pans and utensils also require separate storage.

one for two? Kosher kitchens can double up on appliances, drawers, even sinks. But the Wieners' main sink (above) gets multiple use, requiring faithful maintenance and a prescribed wait between meat and dairy-food contact. Leading kosher certifier Star-K says that sinks fabricated of stainless steel or granite can be made kosher; those made of porcelain, solid surfacing, or china cannot.

narrow victory Though slender, the tall larder cabinet to the left of the ovens (above, left) can store a vast variety of everyday kitchen essentials. With full-extension slides and easy access from two sides, this unit allows users to pack in provisions from top to bottom.

Not to be lost in the welcome infusion of sunlight is an economical kitchen layout. Two or more people can be at work here without having traffic problems, thanks to long stretches of countertop. A person standing at the island need take only a few steps to reach any appliance.

cooking truly light

the most important element in Barry and Alison Braunstein's new kitchen never cost them a penny: natural light. Architect Paul Lukez of Somerville, Massachusetts, emphasized illumination, turning the kitchen addition to the Westin, Massachusetts, 1960s Colonial into a window on the world.

The focal point of the enlarged kitchen is the cooktop, behind which three windows with Frank Lloyd Wright–inspired geometry offer garden vistas. "We placed a large panel of acid-etched copper in the center of the wall, so whoever is preparing a meal could concentrate on cooking but still have side views of the landscape," Lukez explained. "We wrapped the corners in glass for a 3-D look and to take full advantage of the sunlight."

Smaller windows in long, shallow banks on either side of the addition offer snippets of sky, and French doors lead to an inviting patio designed to coordinate with the kitchen. "Each window has its own view and its own story to tell," Lukez said. "The longer you look, the more varied and vibrant the view."

The rest of the kitchen was similarly designed to capitalize on available natural light. Lukez selected an amber-rich color palette, prominent in the cooktop's copper backsplash and the island's granite countertop. The glossy granite, along with the custom stainless steel appliances and exhaust hood, sparkles when the sun shines. The white cabinets and perimeter countertops present a blank canvas that artfully reflects the light. Whether the day is sunny or cloudy, the designer insisted, "the light brings a painterly quality to the space and also adds a whole new, magical dimension."

The Braunsteins like the sunny kitchen so much that they have turned it into the nerve center of the house. Barry, a real-estate lawyer and the family's chief cook, can't wait to fix each "adventurous palate" meal. Alison, a voice-over actress, recently decided to move her computer to her kitchen desk, and the couple's teenage children long ago decided that they simply like to hang out in the space.

"We love to entertain," Barry reported. "When we have elaborate dinner parties, we eat in the formal dining room, but I always set up the bar in the kitchen. It's so much fun to be there that sometimes our guests don't want to leave the kitchen when dinner is served."

LEFT: Two vertical rows of niches add open storage to the wall with the built-in ovens.

BELOW, LEFT: Clerestory windows ensure that light penetrates the kitchen from two sides. Adding to their impact are French doors, which lead out to a patio designed to coordinate with the kitchen's breezy decor.

BOTTOM: The plan suggests that the principal chef, when standing at the cooktop, occupies a kind of kitchen command center.

seize the daylight

With bright natural light in abundance, architect Paul Lukez had to be sure the surfaces he chose would maximize the sunniness and also work well with each other. Here was his strategy:

use reflective colors White cabinets and countertops reflect the sunshine, giving the room a vibrance that darker surfaces would have soaked up.

add complementary hues To avoid having a dull, uninterrupted flow of stark white, the architect introduced amber-themed highlights, notably the copper backsplash (opposite) and granite island top (previous pages).

go glossy Black appliances create another layer of contrast with the cabinets and countertops. But instead of deadening the light, their glossy surfaces provide reflections that add to the overall brilliance of the space.

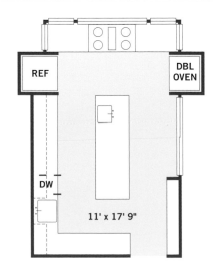

REF

DBL OVEN

DW

11' x 17' 9"

Wrapping windows around the corner essentially provides two views from one spot and takes maximum advantage of the natural light.

roll with it

LEFT: Those are not base cabinets against the wall; they are restaurant-grade stainless steel tables. The designer had mahogany cabinet and drawer boxes built to fit on each worktable shelf.

OPPOSITE: In the island, movable wood drawers expand the amount of top-shelf space that is usable. The deep tones of the mahogany storage components complement the floor, which is made of reclaimed Douglas fir. Window light eases the heaviness of all the dark wood.

ABOVE: In plan, this kitchen is essentially an expanded L with a modest-size island. The room's lack of wall cabinets means there is space for windows that supply much-needed light and ventilation, plus outdoor views.

equipped with a center island and commercial stainless steel appliances plus a double-sink unit, this industrial-style chef's work center has just about everything—except a surfeit of kitchen cabinets.

"The owner wanted an open, urbane kitchen that was highly functional and super-utilitarian, one that would not obstruct views of the woods and river outside," said designer/builder Charles Ferguson, of the Meridian Company in Beaufort, South Carolina. "And he wanted great flexibility."

Ferguson, in turn, added a Greenville architect, Charles Lachanos, to the team. Together, they came up with a low-budget design that really takes the toque. Lachanos took advantage of the kitchen's 14-foot-high walls and turned the 300-square-foot space into a loftlike setting. By putting banks of windows on two of the walls, he complemented the architecture of the shingle-style house and underscored the beauty of the owner's 26-acre property on tranquil Coosaw Island.

"The biggest challenge was finding a place for storage," said Lachanos. "With so many windows in this room, there was no place to put cabinets." So,

Ferguson turned to a kitchen-supply house and substituted rolling stainless steel tables for fixed cabinets. One table has become the 4-by-4-foot central island; others stand side by side, forming a countertop around the kitchen's perimeter. The tables cost no more than $120 each, much less expensive than conventional cabinetry. "They can all be rolled around as needed," Ferguson declared. "When the cook is working, they can be pulled together; when people are eating in the kitchen, the island can be pushed aside and set up as a small table. Even the range can be moved out a few inches from the wall."

To facilitate storage and give the tables a less sterile look, Ferguson specified drawer boxes of dovetailed mahogany, lined with maple, that fit on the shelves of the worktables. The woody warmth complements the wide reclaimed Douglas fir planks of the floor and the stucco fireplace.

Glass shelves mounted within some of the windows form artistic perches for glassware and china, and industrial track lighting can be adjusted to illuminate individual workstations to suit the task at hand. A stand-up mahogany pantry, which

VIEW MINDERS

Ferguson designed to match the table drawers, provides a convenient spot for food storage.

"This design not only shows off kitchen equipment but also fits in with the sculptural nature of the house," Lachanos remarked. "What we produced is eco-friendly—we're not using hardwoods or wasting trees on cabinetry." And should the owner ever decide to move, all he has to do is roll his kitchen into his new home.

ABOVE: One of the kitchen's few fixed elements, the sink and stainless steel stand complete a restaurant-like look. The high arc of the wall-mounted faucet is great for filling tall pots, and the sprayer hose can blast the food residue off those pots—plus all the food-encrusted dishes—when the meal is over.

cutting cabinets

Assembling a kitchen without cabinets may seem implausible, but designer/ builder Charles Ferguson and architect Charles Lachanos figured out a way.

turn the tables The design team effectively transformed restaurant-grade steel tables (left) into contemporary kitchen furniture by outfitting them with variable-size wooden drawers.

wheel the deal The fact that the stainless steel tables are on wheels (below, left) lets the homeowner locate storage where he wants it and move it out of the way when he needs to.

look at things your way Glass shelves (below) provide storage without adding visual bulk, sacrificing light, or compromising the view.

farmhouse modern

"**I really didn't design** this kitchen with a client in mind. I designed it for myself," insisted Laura DuCharme-Conboy, AIA, of DuCharme Architecture in La Jolla, California. The house, too, was her conception, a 3,700-square-foot structure on a site not far from the Pacific Ocean.

"For an architect, this was as much fun as I could ever have," she said. "I was able to ask myself what I would do if given free rein. What materials would I want to play with?"

What she created was a two-story, four-bedroom house that includes a 14-by-20-foot kitchen with Texas limestone on the walls and French limestone on the floor. For her, these natural elements have material integrity. "I chose to use other materials that are straightforward as well: wood beams, wood windows, countertops of lightly honed granite, and cabinets that are either stainless steel or mahogany."

Laura, her husband Garth, and their two young children lived in the house for about three years, then moved on. Another couple, Amanda and Gene Hodges, fell in love with the place, bought it, and moved in with their two youngsters. "I thought the kitchen was really stunning," Amanda exulted. "From the moment I first saw it, it seemed a wonderful place to cook in and an inviting place to sit down in to enjoy a meal. And, like the rest of the house, it's child- and family-friendly."

The centerpiece of the kitchen is a 7½-foot-long table that is both a work island and a dining space. Left behind for the Hodgeses, who loved it, the table is basically a giant slab of Torrey pine laid on slanting mahogany legs. "I was glad to have it stay with the kitchen," said Laura. "The top is smooth—its surface sanded and oiled, of course—but the live edges reflect the actual bumpy curvature of a tree."

The cabinets are a dazzling mix: dark-stained oak on the base units and stainless steel on the console and wall units. "I wanted the kitchen to look like an old European farmhouse with ultra-modern cabinetry," Laura explained.

New owner Amanda immediately claimed the kitchen as her own. "It's not only beautiful but lovely to use. Gene and I couldn't have chosen a nicer place if we'd had it designed for us."

LEFT: A pine-topped table with slightly splayed legs creates a touch of nature—a rough-hewn, angular accent—in the squared-off space of this sleek setting, which is mostly an amalgam of glass, limestone, and stainless steel.

a blend of style and warmth

With stone walls, a stone floor, and a 10½-foot-tall ceiling, this kitchen could have ended up visually cold. It didn't, though. Here's why:

toning down The limestone's soft neutral tones add touches of warmth to the walls and floor (above left).

historical reference Structural beams of dark-stained Douglas fir give the room a sense of solidity plus the illusion of age.

mixing materials Dark-stained oak cabinets balance the lightness of the glass and the sink console's vast expanse of stainless steel.

natural elements A huge custom window trimmed with mahogany draws in sunlight and frames a view of the garden and its exotic bamboo plantings (above right). A fireplace adds a warm glow to the space, along with the candles set in a custom fixture hung over the kitchen table.

color counts Colors in the pendant lights and in a sensitively edited accessory collection underscore the kitchen's inherently welcoming nature.

RIGHT: At one end of the kitchen, opposite the window wall—with its verdant views and influx of sunlight—the element of fire appears. A focal point, particularly after dark, the fireplace cuts into the wall at waist height for optimal impact.

14' X 20'

REF

MW

ABOVE: With windows on one wall framing a garden view and a glass-fronted fireplace shielding flames on another, this kitchen was planned as a subtle salute to the beauty of nature.

vintage advantage

some things are timeless— a signature strand of pearls or the perennial little black dress, for example. Similarly, some designs never go out of style, according to architect Lise Matthews, AIA, ASID, whose modern take on the classic black-and-white service kitchen is shown here. Designed for the owners of a circa-1940 Colonial Revival home located in the Westwood section of Los Angeles, the project posed remodeling challenges for LCM Studios, Matthews's Venice, California–based firm.

Among her client's priorities were reorganizing the kitchen for more efficient cooking and dining, adding a sunny breakfast nook, and introducing a user-friendly layout that bridges the gap between indoors and out.

"Obviously we needed to open the place up," said Matthews, who shifted the kitchen to the rear of the house to capture great outdoor views. Eliminating interior walls and stealing space from a former laundry room resulted in a 195-square-foot space that is twice the size of the original.

Anchored by an island with pull-up seating, the kitchen's crisp, L-shaped open plan flows seamlessly into an expansive family room and, adjacent to it, a sun-splashed 12-by-18-foot breakfast nook.

Windows bring the outdoors inside, thanks in part to the elimination of upper cabinets in favor of cottage-style windows with tilt-out sashes. Instead of a bulky range hood, less intrusive industrial exhaust fans dot the wall above the range. "We passed inspection because the homeowners planned to do most of their cooking on the outdoor grill," Matthews explained. Another focal point is a large, wall-mounted "plaster" sink— a glazed-china unit with an integral backsplash. This configuration, often found in commercial art studios, was a precursor to the apron-front farm sinks that began gaining popularity in the 1990s.

Traditional fixtures and finishes also get a modern twist: Classic subway-tiled counters, stainless steel appliances, and white-painted cabinets with recessed-panel doors play well with hard-wearing, espresso-

LEFT: Linoleum countertops with carefully nailed aluminum edging add a quirky yet practical touch to this kitchen. Fabricated from extra-wide sheets, the tops have no seams.

ABOVE: For added sunlight, windows replace wall cabinets. Because privacy is not an issue, the windows are left unadorned—and open, whenever possible, to admit fresh air.

RIGHT: Both the look and layout of the kitchen help it flow neatly into the breakfast room, where, for continuity, the same flagstone pavers that are used on the patio also line the floor.

stained plank floors. The countertops are a surprise, however, clad in inexpensive marbleized sheet linoleum rather than more-sought-after granite or stone. After a decade of hard use, they still look great, says current owner Amanda Beesley-Weinstock, who relocated from New York in 2004 with her husband, Nicholas, and their three children. Her only caveat: Avoid placing hot objects directly on the surface. "We've only had one accident," she confided, "and it was because we forgot to tell our babysitter how to treat the countertops."

The new owner's favorite spot? The alcove with the sink. Even though she rarely washes dishes by hand, she still enjoys the task. "I can stand here and look out over the lemon and orange trees and watch the kids play," she said. "I couldn't do that in New York."

9'6" X 20'6"

REF

REF

ABOVE: Removing some walls and cribbing space from adjacent rooms created a generous canvas for this L-shaped kitchen and its long island.

design points

Here are the most creative ideas that, all told, give this kitchen a decidedly vintage look:

city lights Mounted on a brick wall, the ceiling lights (top, left) would look like warning signals. In their current context, however, the fixtures' simple geometry creates an elegant counterpoint to the futuristic vibe of the clear, conical pendants (top, right).

porthole vents A pair of in-wall fans (above) hark back to the ventilation installed in urban and suburban homes in the middle of the 20th century.

classic sink This large china sink (right) imparts the requisite classic look, but it is also scaled to deal with any size dish, pot, or pan used in the kitchen.

a glass act

OPPOSITE: The room's single wall cabinet has sliding glass doors that reduce its visual weight and allow it to essentially disappear into the wall that surrounds it, which is all windows.

BELOW: Gutting the kitchen and taking out the partition that separated it from the dining room allowed designer Fu-Tung Cheng to turn what had been a U-shaped kitchen into a spacious galley.

those low-slung homes built in California in the mid-20th century set the precedent for indoor-outdoor living throughout the U.S. One example is this 1960 house in Orinda, whose owners have lived there some 40 years. In 1971 they expanded the house and redid the kitchen. But three decades later, as the garden matured along with the couple's tastes, they wished for even more transparency between the kitchen and their tranquil backyard.

Three of the architects they consulted suggested pushing out an exterior wall—a cost-prohibitive solution, given earthquake-prone California's rigorous building and engineering codes. But Berkeley-based designer Fu-Tung Cheng had other ideas. With a few deft deletions and additions, he created a sparkling

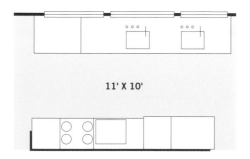

ABOVE: The generous gap between the sides of the galley and the separated single-bowl sinks along the outside wall allow more than one person to function in the kitchen comfortably.

11' X 10'

kitchen that seems to float against the greenery, while leaving its basic footprint intact.

Cheng, who heads up Cheng Design, is known for organic, sculpted lines and a down-to-earth style—exactly the look the wife was after. "I wanted more glass this time and the space itself to be a little edgy, very contemporary, and kind of Zen," she said. Cheng gutted the kitchen and tore out a partition between it and the dining area, replacing the old U-shaped workspace with a long, efficiently organized galley. He also extended a wall about two feet at one end of the room. "The old kitchen didn't have this linear generosity," Cheng declared. "Our idea was to stretch things out."

Another house-opening move was to expand on the rhythm of existing clerestory windows. By filling the entire vertical space between clerestory and countertop with new windows and adding French doors, Cheng created a sweeping wall of glass overlooking the garden. To preserve that view, he omitted upper wall storage except for one linear cabinet clad in reflective glass tiles that hangs above the counter.

On the galley's opposite side, an interior wall was notched out to

allow natural light to reach the living room. Sleek materials bounce light around. The stainless steel backsplash segues into a shelf and a niche for the microwave, and Cheng used his trademark concrete to wrap two end walls and part of the countertops.

For the wife, who described herself as "neurotically neat," purging unused possessions to gain garden views was undeniably worthwhile. "The openness is fabulous," she said. "It makes this part of the house seem bigger."

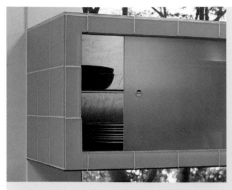

OPPOSITE: Instead of getting an expanded cooktop by installing a super-wide range, this kitchen features a range and, beside it, a separate grill. The non-oven space below the grill provides essential cookware storage.

bright ideas

Abundant natural light makes this kitchen extremely inviting. Designer Fu-Tung Cheng maximized the overall brightness with his clean-line design and the use of an abundant amount of glass and steel.

■ The back of the glass-fronted wall cabinet is also translucent (top, far left), giving the box a pleasing glow. The glass-tile sides and front frame accentuate the gleaming effect.

■ Concrete and stone countertops (top, left) have a sheen that helps reflect all that soothing California sunshine.

■ A high-arc polished chrome faucet (center, far left) adds elegance and a bonus glint of brightness.

■ A stool is tucked away in a handy nook (bottom, far left) under the single drawer next to the sink.

■ The door hardware and wire shelves of the pull-out pantry (center, left) also gleam in the light, but the decision to order these items in metal, not wood, was made mainly for stylistic and ease-of-maintenance reasons.

■ Steel rods set into the countertop near a sink comprise a built-in drainboard (bottom, left). This largely eliminates any need for a dish rack, which would have added clutter to the countertop.

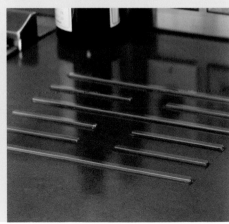

color
and shine

The secret of the success of traditional oil paintings extends beyond the artists' choice of subject matter; it often lies in their skilled use of light. This is similarly true in kitchen design. Although scale and space-use are equally important, what often completes the way a kitchen looks and functions is the role light plays—sunlight as well as ambient and task lighting. A designer's color palette is also a factor in defining space and giving it specific focus. But what color inevitably needs to achieve a desired effect is...light.

bull's-eye reckoning

OPPOSITE: Like a target, this room is light around the edges and dark in the center, but that welcome contrast is only part of its appeal. Note how the island countertop turns down at a 90-degree angle. The lighted niche at the end is actually one of three that show off a rotating selection of the owners' collectibles.

hungry for a fresh look in a home now free of children, Sheri and Mark Christopherson of Ellsworth, Wisconsin, were determined to have a kitchen that would help them make the most of being empty-nesters. "It was about time for us to take the plunge," Sheri stated. "We'd been in our home for 25 years and hadn't updated any of it since we moved in. We wanted to bring in a lot more style."

Along with a clean, contemporary look and a vaulted ceiling, the couple had an island and a built-in eating area high on their remodeling wish list. Sheri pored over design magazines, clipping photos for her idea file, unsure if space would permit the eating area she was so eager to have.

Jean-Claude Desjardins, of the Apple Valley, Minnesota, design studio Belle Kitchen, solved the problem: He made room for a banquette by removing a large corner closet. ("It was really just a big catchall for junk," said Sheri.) Dropping windows into the former closet's outer walls, he made the corner an inviting spot for a compact custom table with a sandblasted glass top in the shape of a slightly rounded wedge.

It was exactly what the room needed. "The way our old kitchen was situated,

we had a peninsula bar," Sheri recalled, "and what ended up happening was, I never got to sit down while the kids were growing up; I ate most of my meals standing at the counter. Now that the kids are gone and there's not such a mad rush, Mark and I can relax and enjoy mealtimes. The point is: We didn't want to always have to sit at our large dining room table; we wanted something cozier. We also wanted the eating area because we didn't want to get into the nasty habit of eating in the living room or even our family room."

Desjardins's other masterstroke was the kitchen's asymmetrical island. The end facing the eating area is curved to mirror the banquette table; the two opposing curves define the widest possible pathway through the tight space. At the other end of the island, facing the dining room, the granite countertop takes a 90-degree turn downward to the floor. Openings cut in the stone frame three lighted display shelves, which make jewel-box settings for a rotating display of pieces from the Christophersons' sculpture collection.

Desjardins's design partner, Tricia Bayer, selected Indian tropical-green granite for the island's countertop whose base is built of rich-toned

cherry. In contrast, the perimeter cabinets are a light maple; for them, Bayer specified counters and a backsplash of golden Juparana granite.

"At first," said Sheri, " I was leery of using different woods and granites, but I love the result. Red speckles in the green granite pick up the burgundy color of the island, while the lighter granite blends with the maple cabinets to keep the island the focal point. But up close, you can still appreciate the beauty of the stone."

As for the vaulted ceiling the couple wanted, Desjardins didn't need to raise the roof; he just removed the ceiling, opened up the overhead crawl space, and installed two skylights. The daylight they bring in is supplemented by high-tech monorail pendants, recessed ceiling fixtures, and under-cabinet lights. ("We had some fun with the lighting," Sheri commented with a chuckle.) The three components can be mixed and matched for plenty of task lighting as well as artfully subdued nighttime effects.

This lighting balance paired with a deft use of pale and dark colors is largely responsible for the success of the redesign, making an efficient kitchen a beautiful, inviting space.

LEFT: This cozy, comfortable, light-filled eating nook with curved-glass tabletop and cushy seating was once a large, windowless closet.

BELOW: Behind this panel is a mechanical conduit. The panel itself could have been wasted space but for the custom-designed utensil rack.

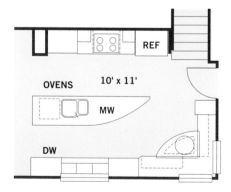

ABOVE: Because of her kitchen's new design, Sheri Christopherson feels encouraged to sit down for casual meals with her husband, Mark, instead of simply standing at a peninsula.

LEFT: Gold-tinged Juparana granite on the cooktop-area counter picks up the lighter tones of the maple cabinets. In the foreground, red flecks in the Indian tropical-green granite help that surface complement the color of the island's cherry base cabinetry.

design points

■ An oversize closet oddly situated in one corner of the kitchen was a magnet for clutter. Fitted with new windows, the space functions far more sensibly now as a dining banquette. Thanks to its curved outer edge, the wedge-shaped tabletop does not protrude into the primary traffic path.

■ Cut into one end of the island, lighted niches hold a rotating display of artwork that can be seen clearly and appreciated from the dining room.

■ Flooring of 12-by-24-inch porcelain tiles, rather than the more typical 12-inch squares, minimizes busy, worrisome grout lines and echoes the decorative grid of wood strips on the outside of the island.

■ Shallow spice shelves built into the granite backsplash and a custom utensil rack on a cabinet panel that conceals a mechanical conduit make attractive storage solutions.

grown-up galley

with one glaring exception,

the 2,800-square-foot Edwardian home on a hilly lot in a San Francisco suburb seemed to have it all—a prime location, a lush backyard, and enough of its original 1908 detailing to captivate the new owner, a single mom with a growing child. But the poorly laid-out kitchen and its cheap 1970s cabinets and laminate counters were not the homeowner's taste. And the narrow galley shape was much too cramped for two cooks to maneuver in, making it hard for mother and daughter to do what they love to do—bake together.

Adding to the congestion, a hulking peninsula awkwardly divided the work zone from a snug sitting area with a fireplace at the opposite end of the room. "The mantel consumed most of the space," the owner recalled. "There was just room for a couch, and I wanted more of a connection between the two areas." Feeling challenged, she called in designers Gioi Tran and Vernon Applegate, of Applegate Tran Interiors in San Francisco.

Because the room couldn't be altered structurally, Tran and Applegate worked within its long, narrow footprint, stripping walls down to the studs and filling every square inch

with small-space solutions. Along one wall, sleek blond anigre wood cabinetry hides storage and built-in appliances, including a refrigerator, wall oven, microwave, and, at the owner's request, a steam oven. ("It's fantastic because we eat a lot of vegetables," she confided.)

The opposite wall holds a long, distressed black granite countertop that wraps around a stainless steel sink and six-burner cooktop. Shelves above and drawers below the counter supply more storage. For a clean, uncluttered look, the flush-front units rise to the ceiling and the hardware is minimal—cut into the bottom of each door of upper cabinets. "We wanted the cabinets to look like wood paneling, which is more space-enhancing," Tran explained.

To improve traffic flow, a shallow, 42-inch-high granite-topped peninsula was installed. "I'm tall, so its height is ideal," the owner said. Below and to the right of the peninsula, the designers built in a toe-kick drawer, which hides a folding stepstool that boosts the daughter up to counter height. "It's a great use of otherwise wasted space, and that ladder is handy for reaching the top shelves," the owner insisted.

Instead of parking a couple of barstools at the peninsula, Tran and

Applegate combined two functions by installing a storage bench under the window on the opposite wall. "The low bench keeps the room open and airy, provides a great storage opportunity, and is a perfect perch for guests when visiting with the cook," said Tran.

The bench also creates a transition to the sitting area, which gained space when a flush fireplace replaced the old bulky mantel. An earthy palette of cream walls, natural-colored stone, and heavily grained oak flooring unifies the two spaces. But judicious jolts of color and gleaming stainless steel were also woven in to create visual excitement. "This may not be the biggest kitchen, but it's got everything I need," the owner boasted. "It's efficient, a joy to cook in, and I love to show it off."

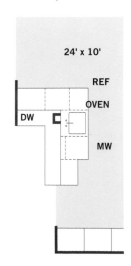

24' x 10'

REF

OVEN

DW

MW

LEFT: Cabinets on the appliance wall subtly shrink in depth, a taper that creates a healthy distance between the peninsula and bench seating.

BELOW: A narrow floor-to-ceiling wine rack set into the appliance wall is a handy amenity, even though it contains bottles of carbonated water—the owner stores wine elsewhere. The open shelves also provide visual relief from what otherwise would be a massive cabinetry wall.

OPPOSITE: A trio of richly colored drawer panels below the cooktop holds pots and pans and repeats the wood tone on the base of the peninsula. The tambour door covering shallow shelves in the adjacent wall is in the same finish as the custom stainless steel vent hood.

make the most of minimal space

- Avoid using too many colors, patterns, and materials. Tran and Applegate chose a mostly neutral scheme to make the space seem larger. To avoid a busy look, they limited the materials they used and repeated them throughout the space. For example, brushed metal elements, including the sink and faucet (right), recur in the sofa legs. Even the faux-painted walls echo the cabinets' striated wood grain.

- Add storage where you can. Here, storage capacity was more than doubled via ceiling-height cabinets, a toe-kick drawer (below, right), a dual-purpose bench, and a ceiling-high wine rack at one end of the appliance wall.

- De-clutter your countertops. An appliance garage over the peninsula (below, center) keeps the mixer and other small appliances close at hand but out of sight. Similarly, a spice niche behind a roll-up stainless steel door to the right of the cooktop (opposite) keeps the countertop clear.

The dining table is strategically placed between the kitchen and the door to the backyard barbecue. A wine refrigerator makes retrieving a bottle of cool Chardonnay an easy chore. Note the glass shelving set into the window: It's great for showing off colorful items, easily reached.

playing the angles

compared to its neighbors, Barbara Tarmy's Bridgehampton, New York, home was small and bland. The houses around it had been designed by a renowned architect, the late Norman Jaffe. Tarmy's was a spec house from the 1980s covered in old cedar shingles. When she decided to fix it up, she and architect Carl Finer, of Elterman Finer Architects in New York City, discovered how slapdash her place really was. "It was not well built at all," Finer said grimly. "For example, the building paper had been put on backwards, which meant that rain could actually leak in."

Tarmy specifically asked Finer to produce an exciting kitchen space for her family, which included husband Gary Fradin and two growing children. "The kitchen is the first thing you see when you walk in," she said. "I told Carl he could be really creative. I was happy to give him carte blanche."

Finer came back with the total opposite of what a previous pro had recommended. "That designer wanted to install familiar-looking white-painted cabinets," Finer recalled. "My thought was, "Let's have some fun with this. Why should we fight modern geometry and the very nature of the architecture?" His solution was strikingly geometric and called for an imaginative use of color.

On the cabinets, dyed veneers show off festive shades of blue, green, and yellow. A peninsula with a sink extends into the kitchen at an angle, and a wedge of blue lays over the green panel at the end of the extension. "The outside of this house has your typical weathered white cedar shingles—very monochromic," Finer said. "Then you come inside and—surprise—it's not staid or traditional but a very vibrant, very whimsical series of spaces."

A stainless steel hood over the commercial-style range adds another geometric element to the kitchen. Countertops in stainless steel and cork provide visual counterpoints; copious windows bring in sunshine; and a glass shelf suspended along the middle of a wall of windows creates interest and storage without blocking the light.

The kitchen opens to the living room and dining room. "It's a family space," Finer pointed out. "And there's room enough for friends to help out with the cooking." For more than one cook, the kitchen includes a second sink, on a second peninsula. One sink is dedicated to washing, the other to food

OPPOSITE: A commercial-style range occupies its own niche, topped by a starkly contemporary exhaust hood—which extends outward, a wedge of stainless steel.

BELOW: Even in the smallest details, geometry is a dominant presence in this kitchen. Tiny cylindrical drawer pulls play off the triangular cutouts that let owners open cupboard doors.

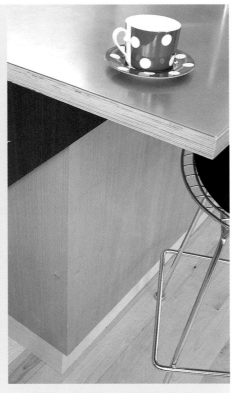

prep. "It's incredibly practical," Tarmy insisted. "I can rinse off dishes and literally turn around to the other sink to clean vegetables. Two people can work here comfortably—and that's generally with one of our dogs at our feet."

Tarmy enjoys shopping at local farms in eastern Long Island for eggs, meat, and produce in season. Now she has a kitchen that's as fresh—and colorful—as the ingredients she brings home.

insider tips

counter intelligence Leaving all the edges of the metal-topped counters unwrapped exposes their many layers of laminated wood (above) and complements the way the material is used throughout this kitchen.

roll play Creating deep drawers for dishes (above, left) reduces the number of wall cabinets needed.

light on Low-voltage track lighting systems (left) are flexible design elements—literally. Each rail can be bent and shaped to bring task lighting to where it is undeniably needed.

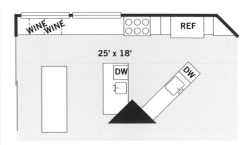

ABOVE: Angles figure prominently, and practically, in the floor plan of the kitchen. Installing sinks and dishwashers in adjacent counters raised the convenience quotient for anyone doing prep and cleanup tasks, as both pairings are within easy reach.

dream design for a pro

none of the hallmarks of 1970s design—sunken living room, shag carpeting, ceilings textured like cottage cheese—posed a deterrent for David Gingrass, who was confident he could turn his 1,500-square-foot house in Napa, California, into something befitting modern times. Chef-owner of the San Francisco restaurant Two, Gingrass proved to be just as skillful in the workshop as he is at the range. Doing most of the renovation himself, he created a home that more than met his personal and professional needs.

Down came interior walls, as rooms were reordered and the place took on the characteristics of a contemporary ranch house: open spaces, large light-admitting windows, easy outdoor access. To gain even more space, he also removed closets and jettisoned a pantry. As he never deals with packaged or prepared foods, he felt no pantry was needed. He also absorbed a space that had contained the home laundry and, in a distant corner of the attached garage, found another spot for his washer and dryer.

Gingrass wanted his kitchen to be a kind of dining theater, a place to entertain as well as work. Two walls were removed, opening the space up to the foyer and the adjacent dining room. At 120 square feet, the new kitchen, he said, "is roughly the size of the old one and in the same general part of the house, but it bears no resemblance to what had been there before."

The new kitchen's amenities are state-of-the-art but less than lavish, somewhat surprising considering that this is the realm of a successful professional chef. Two ovens and a microwave are built into one wall, a six-burner cooktop dominates the island, and a dishwasher is conveniently placed near a large undermount sink on a wall where a frameless window is also the backsplash. The only visual indication that this is the domain of a cooking professional is the kitchen's restaurant-style refrigerator-freezer.

The custom cabinets Gingrass chose are made of wenge, a hardwood from central Africa. Those mounted above the window have acrylic insets in the doors. "White linen was fused into the resin to add a textural element," he pointed out. "I wanted dark wood for the cabinets, but not too much of it. Having those translucent door panels lightens things up a lot."

Other contrasts include stainless steel countertops and appliances, plus an island made of medium-density fiberboard (MDF) that was given a reddish-orange lacquer finish. Gingrass insisted that over and above wipeable surfaces, abundant light, and an inviting open-space plan, the single most important amenity in kitchen design should be "maximum flexibility." And this kitchen definitely has it.

ABOVE: A butcher-block cutting board rests near the stainless steel sink, which is skillfully fused to the steel countertop, creating the look of an uninterrupted one-piece installation.

OPPOSITE: With the dining table just steps away from the cooking island, guests enjoy not only freshly made meals but also a close-up view of the way Chef Gingrass prepares them.

LEFT: Neutral stainless steel countertops are offset by earth tones—including the red, yellow, and orange glass tiles that form the backsplash. The hood over the built-in cooktop has a railed shelf that holds condiments, utensils, and "even my car keys and cell phone," said Gingrass.

ABOVE: Storage add-ons are plentiful in all the kitchen cabinets. Swing-out shelving in the corner provides access to mixing bowls, baking dishes, and some small appliances. Also shown here is the zebra-wood floor—with its dark, heavy grain—which the homeowner laid down after ripping out the old kitchen's dated vinyl.

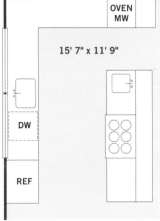

ABOVE: To acquire the open space he wanted, Gingrass pulled down walls and eliminated the pantry. Having done that, he arranged all the elements so that—as a chef and potential host—he could manage effortlessly in the new kitchen.

OPPOSITE: This table is not just for dining. It also serves as a place for guests to gather when Gingrass is preparing food or even cleaning up. The benches at either end relieve any visual clutter and, as needed, will seat extra guests.

a pro's priorities

A high-powered range is just one ingredient in a restaurant-style kitchen. Here's what makes this residential space work for an actual working pro:

good things come in twos

The kitchen has two sinks—one for cooking and one for washing pots and cleaning up (above). In addition to a high-arched gooseneck faucet, Gingrass installed a flexible, movable pot filler. He also stacked two wall ovens below the built-in microwave on one wall (above, left), and the cooktop on his island features two large, high-powered burners (previous page).

restaurant style, home fit

The chef's giant two-door refrigerator (previous page) looks commercial and contains a vast amount of storage. But its 22-inch depth was designed specifically for a residential kitchen.

steeling home
Generous use of stainless steel countertops (above and above, left) simplifies cleanup. Butcher-block boards facilitate chopping duties.

a place for everything
Drawer dividers keep kitchen tools organized. This split-level insert (above) makes maximum use of the drawer depth.

california compromise

OPPOSITE: Eliminating wall cabinets let the owners room to install a big-screen TV and a piece of African artwork. Blue paint provides a cool counterpoint to the rest of the room.

BELOW: A bank of cabinets framing the double ovens and warming drawer compensate for storage lost when the designers made so many of the kitchen's wall cabinets disappear.

bay area homeowners Paula Groves and Johnny Hawthorne had a long list of kitchen desires that seemed maddeningly conflicted. They wanted an open space that would also be separated from adjacent rooms. They coveted lots of amenities and copious storage, but they didn't want their kitchen to look overly busy.

To mold these far-flung ideas into a coherent space, the couple turned to Vernon Applegate and Gioi Tran, of Applegate Tran Interiors in San Francisco. They had collected "a gigantic album of pictures from every magazine you can think of," Hawthorne recalled. "We didn't put anything in the album that didn't illustrate ideas we both favored," said Groves. They settled on an African-Asian blend, a fusion sparked by unfussy lines and neutral colors.

The old kitchen in their Oakland, California, home was a small galley, completely isolated from the rest of the house. Into this, the couple envisioned adding a 48-inch cooktop, multiple sinks, a built-in refrigerator, a big-screen TV, and lots of storage— all without a lot of visual clutter. "Wow, I think you're asking for a lot," Tran remembered saying. "We were

compelled to tell Paula and Johnny that they would have to give up something. They ultimately decided they were willing to lose the den to get a bigger kitchen." Indeed, the designers grafted the den/family room onto the existing kitchen, creating a total remodeled space measuring 10 by 22 feet.

The area gained from this annexation allowed Applegate and Tran to add the amenities Groves and Hawthorne requested. However, the true challenge was beefing up the kitchen's storage capacity without overwhelming the space. Sacrificing upper cabinets effectively eliminated bulk. To make up for lost storage, the designers dedicated an entire end wall to flush-front cabinetry fitted around a pair of wall ovens and a warming drawer.

Some design flourishes make the stretch of clean wall impressive. One is a stainless steel vent hood that extends along an entire run of base cabinets, forming a modernist hearth of sorts. Other features are a piece of African art and a flat-screen TV. The most remarkable aspect of the wall, however, is its color—blue. With all the neutral, earthy colors, Tran said, "we thought, 'Let's contrast that with a cool tone on the wall.' But at first our clients weren't

too keen on blue." In the end, however, he convinced them: "We didn't want the TV to jump out at them when it wasn't on—think about a white wall with a blank black screen on it. Also, if they really didn't like it, we could repaint."

Structural issues also posed challenges. Above the kitchen is a loft supported by columns that had to stay put. The designers built an island around one of the columns. "The island creates a barrier," Tran explained. "The

BELOW: Two sinks on generous spans of countertop reinforce the fact that this is a kitchen where multiple cooks can function as comfortably as one. The wide aisle between counters allows traffic to flow smoothly.

BELOW, TOP RIGHT: Exposed edges add texture and interest to pressed-wood cabinet doors and drawers. The easy-grip handles are brushed stainless steel.

elegant blend and balance

Whether it's the materials in the space or the people in the home, this kitchen idealizes the hoped-for harmony of everyday life. Designers Vernon Applegate and Gioi Tran paired convenience and aesthetics to create a very satisfying kitchen environment. Here's how:

establishing a mood Earth tones and neutrals dominate the space (the blue wall being the primary exception). The cabinets have a fairly tight wood grain that runs horizontally for a change of pace (left). In addition to highlighting the slightly washed-out oak, dark stain rubbed into the wood's surface crevices picks up on the Absolute Black granite countertops. "We decided that if the horizontal surfaces were made dark, the oak cabinets would get more emphasis," Tran explained. The rich, mahogany-stained floor is also oak.

give them a metal The earth-tone palette complements stainless steel, which is featured prominently in the appliances, exhaust hood, and tambour garage door (right, center).

come in, but stay out As part of an open plan, only an island separates the kitchen from the living and dining areas. Thanks to that island's L shape, when someone is cooking, people in the living room can grab a beverage from the wine chiller or refresh a tepid cup of coffee at the microwave (right), all without setting foot in the kitchen proper.

result is an open-plan kitchen—but with some separation."

Groves admitted to experiencing "bumps along the way," including a few government hassles and construction code changes late in the game. She said it smoothed things considerably that she and Hawthorne teamed up well with the designers and their contractor, Jim Crone of Turlock, California. "I don't look at it as a frustrating process," she said. "It was extremely educational."

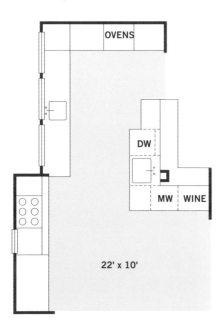

ABOVE: Appropriating space from what had been an adjacent den allowed the designers to convert a galley kitchen into an open-plan suite, with the L-shaped island acting as a kind of half wall creating a sense of separation within the expanded space.

barn-design showcase

"a major challenge in creating a Design Showcase to present at the national Kitchen/Bath Industry Show was to include a notable mix of natural and natural-looking elements," according to Paul Radoy, manager of design services for cabinetmaker Merillat. "Our project had dark, light, and white hardwood cabinets, quartz countertops, a woodlike floor, realistic-looking faux-stone wall segments, and grained-wood trim—all playing off a dominant green tone that enabled us to present a truly contemporary look."

Designer Ingrid Leess pointed out, however, that "the green we used is not all the same. None of it really matches, but it's all complementary. Different shades of green create a lively effect, much more vibrant and interesting than a uniform tone—sort of like the different greens you see in nature."

Green-stained cypress appears as trim throughout, principally on the huge sliding door, framed by a stone doorway, that separates the showcase kitchen and bath areas. "Stone adds texture, character, and warmth, especially when juxtaposed with very graphic, colorful fabrics in what might otherwise be fairly traditional spaces," said Leess. Most of the 600-square-foot

showcase is absorbed by the kitchen, which includes a built-in banquette, a coffee corner, a wine bar, and at least three meal-preparation zones, including a butcher block–topped cart that can be rolled anywhere in the kitchen or out to a patio or deck or wherever else it might be needed.

The quartz-surfaced center island, which offers multiple work spaces, is on two levels. The sink dominates the lower level, which is about 3 inches under the 39-inch height of the upper surface. "Adding those extra inches helped us create a kind of shield," said Nellie Ondrovick, a Merillat interior designer. "If there are dirty dishes in and around the sink, you wouldn't have to look at them while sitting at the table in the dining area. And from that particular vantage point, the countertop becomes a kind of art piece in the way it almost seems to float."

In plan, this showcase kitchen has two contiguous work triangles: from refrigerator to sink to wall ovens, and from ovens to sink to cooktop. Placed directly above the built-in convection oven is a combination steam-and-convection oven, which lets you use either process (or both) and tailor the heating mode to each dish you cook.

Mounted under the sink is a waste disposer; to the left, a dishwasher. Anyone standing at the sink is at the functioning heart of this kitchen's command center, with storage cabinets and drawers, appliances, and myriad work surfaces all within easy reach. The stainless steel cookware is formulated specifically to function on the sleek surface of the induction cooktop. Mounted above it, a spare, understated but highly powerful 48-inch-wide exhaust hood more than meets the demands of sophisticated modern-day gourmet cooking.

BELOW: A professional-style steam/convection oven is installed directly above a single oven; both are built into white cabinets that line the far wall. Awning-style doors on upper cabinets are translucent, so only the shapes and colors of items stored on the shelves within are visible.

BELOW, RIGHT: Drawer storage to the immediate left of the cooktop is fitted out specifically to hold cookware, gadgets, and tableware in various sizes.

BOTTOM, RIGHT: The butcher block–topped steel cart has utensil and cutlery drawers, a highly accessible storage shelf, and a wide steel rod where towels and tablecloths can be draped.

OPPOSITE: Green glass tile forms a sparkling backsplash behind the quartz countertop that wraps three sides of the kitchen. Pendants and track lights supplement bright sunlight pouring in through windows flanking the induction cooktop and its special stainless steel cookware.

spatial efficiency

There's an old adage, known throughout the design world, that it's not the amount of space you have that's important; it's how you use it. In kitchen design, even lavish spaces must be handled wisely, to optimize every inch. However, most remodelers are challenged by small, poorly organized kitchens and must strive to make them work on many levels—for meal making, serving and cleanup, and as gathering spots for visiting family and friends. As you will see, this is a big order that only gifted visionaries can deliver.

reshaping a shell

OPPOSITE: This small space still has room for a wine captain next to the drawers on the left side. This was important for the owner, an enthusiastic collector of fine wines.

BELOW: The flat glass cooktop does not protrude into the limited space the way a standard gas or heavy restaurant-style cooktop would. The side grill, which has its own cover, is similarly unobtrusive.

a lackluster kitchen is what Sarah Gunnels faced when she moved into her home in Boston. The room was nothing more than a builder's special: generic white appliances, white laminate cabinets and counters, hardwood floor. The space, though relatively efficient, was totally out of character with the 150-year-old building, which was located in the historic Back Bay neighborhood.

"The way the apartment is arranged, the kitchen is the first thing you see when you walk through my front door," she reported. "I wanted to do something with it right away but decided to live with it awhile, until I found out exactly what my needs would be."

Gunnels enjoys entertaining and has a starter collection of fine wines. She discovered very quickly she needed more storage space—specifically, to keep serving pieces and packaged foods as well as wine. She also wanted her kitchen to be welcoming, since its location was so prominent. For help she turned to Rosemary Porto, an interior designer with Poggenpohl in Boston, whose specialty is kitchens and baths.

"Sarah wanted her kitchen to look contemporary but have the same warm feeling that pervaded other rooms in her apartment," said her designer. "I worked within the existing space, using the same lighting plan, the same flooring and the same placement of plumbing and appliances." However, she did so while giving this U-shaped kitchen an all-new look. In place of white laminate, Porto had tinted-maple recessed-panel cabinets installed, running them up to nearly ceiling height on two sides of the kitchen. "I took away all the back-wall cabinets," she explained. "I wanted that wall to have the impact of art so that anyone entering the apartment would see it."

Now commanding that wall is a gleaming stainless steel–and–glass exhaust hood mounted against a backsplash of limestone and mosaic tile that extends out on either side, under the upper cabinets. Appliances are new, and, according to Porto, "there are two tall pantries—one next to the refrigerator and one next to the built-in wall ovens and microwave."

Although there are fewer cabinets, Gunnels actually has 25 percent more storage space than before. How? For one thing, there is no longer any dead space in the corners of the room. Instead, there is a hinged unit for serving-pieces that swings outward when the left-hand

corner base-cabinet door is opened. Inside the cabinet, in the opposite corner, is a half lazy Susan, which holds small appliances and other gear that gets only occasional use. Simplicity and elegance prevail, and, the designer boasted, "the new kitchen has a bit of an old-world look."

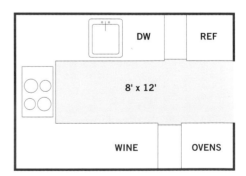

ABOVE: Although adhering largely to the existing plan, designer Porto packed storage into almost every free spot of this U shape. She made minimal use of upper cabinets, however, which makes the space feel less crowded.

OPPOSITE: Mosaic tiles repeat the back wall's harlequin pattern in trim that extends between rows of limestone tiles under wall cabinets.

BELOW, LEFT: Porto's tile design creates an elegant backsplash behind the undermount sink.

BOTTOM, LEFT TO RIGHT: A warming drawer separates the two wall ovens; swing-out wire shelving gives the corner base cabinet optimum accessibility; an undercounter wine cooler contains some of Sarah's fine wines.

in small spaces, just think big

Here's how designer Rosemary Porto added more storage and work space within the existing shell of a U-shaped apartment kitchen:

- New wall-hung cabinets (opposite) are shallower than the old ones, making more counter depth accessible for meal-prep purposes.

- The wall cabinets rise to within 8 inches of the 10-foot-tall ceiling.

- Two built-in pantries have space for long-term storage: barware and crystal on the left, packaged foods on pull-out shelving on the right (opposite).

- Corner cabinets (below, center) are fitted out to prevent dead space.

- A floor-level drawer tucked under the wall ovens was designed to hold cookie sheets and large trays.

filling a tall order

competing purposes came to a head in this kitchen remodeling when the designer wanted to create a feeling of spaciousness and the homeowner insisted on gaining storage—both in a room that would have to stretch mightily to clear 100 square feet. Fortunately, the head they came to—an impressive monolith of a tall pantry—is also the anchor of the entire kitchen.

Designer Tracey Kessler, of TKID, Inc., in San Francisco, had worked for homeowner Linda Hanson before, yet the kitchen in this Capitola, California, beach retreat presented Kessler with a true conundrum: how to marry her kitchen design with the look and feel of the rest of the house. For example, the other rooms featured low, constricting ceilings, as opposed to the comparatively cavernous ceiling in the kitchen. In addition, a wall separated the kitchen from the rest of the house.

"The important thing was to make it feel a little more roomy," Hanson declared. Dealing with space was Kessler's major challenge. In the course of a whole-house renovation, she chose darker colors for the rest of the rooms, but after taking down the dividing wall—a no-brainer when it came to commandeering more square footage—she opted for a beech color in the kitchen. This sandy tone, evident in the cabinets and countertops and on the wall, served to create a feeling of openness in the kitchen and the adjoining areas.

That was easy. Then came the difficult moves. To gain some breathing room, Kessler decided to wipe the upper cabinets completely off one kitchen wall. This idea was not a popular one with the homeowner. "Linda loves storage and she loves storage gadgets," Kessler said. "She couldn't understand what I was doing, but to make this tiny kitchen look larger, I had to free up that space."

The ensuing dispute gave rise to the giant pantry. "Tracey did not want cabinets above the counter on that wall," Hanson explained, "but I needed some storage capability there. As a compromise, she suggested installing cabinetry that wasn't too deep and was contained to the back wall."

The cabinet Kessler designed, with its steel-framed acrylic doors, extends all the way up to the ceiling. Wood panels on the back walls as well as each side of the pantry help these translucent doors blend in with the anigre cabinets in the rest of the kitchen.

Linda Hanson fills the readily reachable parts of her tall built-in pantry with everyday dishes. What is stowed on upper shelves gets used only when guests plan to visit, but because these dishes are so colorful, she likes them visible. Linda uses a stepladder, not the stool, to reach topmost shelves.

BELOW: The peninsula stands opposite the range, refrigerator, and microwave. It replaced a wall that once separated the kitchen from the rest of the house. Removing that wall gave the kitchen and adjoining spaces room to breathe.

BELOW: This cabinet-free wall provoked a debate that led to design of the tall pantry. The pre-existing half-moon upper window might have been enlarged if there had been more time, but it still adds a welcome dollop of natural light.

Hanson fills the towering cabinet easily, even though she spends time at the house only on weekends. "I have some colorful dishes that I use when company comes over, and I really like how they look through the translucent doors," she said. "The dishes I use on a regular basis are stored on the lower, more conveniently accessible shelves in the cabinet." (She uses a stepladder to reach the top shelves.)

As for the nitty-gritty aspects of the kitchen, Hanson explained matter-of-factly that she requested some of the same appliances that she had in

BELOW: The ceiling in the kitchen is much higher than those in other rooms—note the lower ceiling line creeping in from the adjacent room at the upper left corner. Storage in high cabinets helps compensate for the room's small size.

BELOW: In addition to the drawer dishwasher, the cleanup center features one of Hanson's favorite kitchen features: the small arched faucet that is actually an instant hot-water dispenser. She uses it to make tea right out of the tap.

the hang of it Items that perform multiple tasks while taking up minimal space are particularly smiled upon in small kitchens. Take the European-designed hanging rails affixed to the walls over the countertop in the back of the kitchen. Among the available accessories that hang on the rail is a row of hooks to hold cooking utensils (below). Another module holds a roll of paper towels; another holds a supply of coffee filters.

hard decision Initial plans called for a concrete countertop. As homeowner Hanson occasionally lends her home to friends, however, the thinking went that one spilled glass of wine could lead to a ruined countertop and, perhaps, a ruined friendship. So she and designer Tracey Kessler opted for less porous granite counters (right).

her primary residence. She became decidedly more animated, however, on the subject of the instant hot water dispenser. "You can literally brew tea right out of that faucet," she burbled. "That I just love! I'm a big tea drinker."

Tea is a fitting tonic for this space, because Hanson, like many people, considers the beverage a pick-me-up. In this kitchen, as both designer and homeowner found out, up was most definitely the way to go.

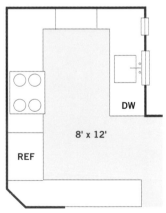

ABOVE: Tiny spaces don't generally allow for much radical reconfiguring, although designer Kessler did manage to take out one wall and rob another of its upper cabinets. The ceiling-high pantry is on the far wall, beyond the range.

a significant merger

OPPOSITE: The kitchen's terrazzo floor gleams in the sunlight; its colors bridge the tones of the wood used in the room, and its pattern contrasts nicely with the wood's linear grains.

"we had separate spaces—
kitchen, breakfast room, and dining room —when we bought this house," says Peg Bausch, CEO of Johnny Grey, Inc., the San Francisco–based North American headquarters of the cutting edge British designer's global firm. What Bausch and husband, Gregory Rodriques, bought was a 46-year-old Spanish-style home on Alameda island, an easy commute to Bay Area offices.

The 2,500-square-foot house was the right size for the couple and their two young children, except that the spaces were cut up (too many doors and doorways) and the rooms felt confined. Working with architectural designer Kevin Hackett, design director of Johnny Grey, they easily removed walls and replaced windows. But the kitchen remained the ultimate challenge.

At 10½ by 11½ feet, it felt squarish. So did the 7-by-11½-foot breakfast room and 10-by-14-foot dining room. "Living in that kitchen was like being stuck in a square that had been cut into three squares," Bausch remembered. "I couldn't see one room from another. I felt completely cut off."

Opening up the space was tricky, as load-bearing headers had to be installed to replace some structural walls. Then other issues surfaced. "For me, light is critical," Bausch declared, encouraged by the fact that her kitchen and the rooms adjoining it had large, symmetrically placed windows. "We kept the same openings but replaced the old windows. The problem was that light wasn't shared; it didn't flow from one space to any other."

Kevin Hackett knew precisely how to address this problem. He created a 400-square-foot active living zone, a Johnny Grey concept that included not just the kitchen, breakfast bar, and built-in banquette but also a dining area and work space. Hackett's new design featured tight circles and sweeping curves. A full range of materials was put to use: terrazzo on the floor, honed granite on countertops, tile and cork on the walls, glass on the banquette table, recycled polymer on the breakfast bar, brushed stainless steel on appliances and trim, and six different woods.

The kitchen's floor plan is an extended U-shape, and there is a viable work triangle, but the details of Hackett's design are what make this kitchen singular. At one end of the peninsula is a raised sphere topped with a slab of pressed concrete with a grooved border—for drainage into a

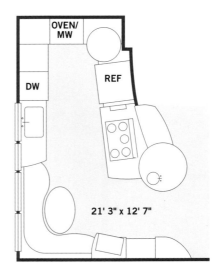

ABOVE: The old squarish kitchen was isolated from other rooms. The new floor plan is more fluid, integrating dining, cooking, and desk-bound activities in one organized open space.

BELOW: At the tip of the peninsula is a removable chopping block crafted of end-grain heart ash. It's ideally positioned in the kitchen's work zone, and, Bausch pointed out, "I can lift and carry it to bring vegetables to the sink."

BELOW: Storage drawers and open shelves, all in elegant figured ash, frame the message center, which is wired for the TV as well as the computer; the latter is accessible when a drawer front is pulled down to become a desk.

BOTTOM: The new kitchen absorbed about 3 feet of the old dining room. Flooring defines the two areas: 18-inch terrazzo tiles in the kitchen, separated from the stained-oak dining area by a stainless steel strip. Stools pull up to a breakfast bar made of translucent recycled polymer.

round undermount sink. Overhead, a circular stainless steel pot rack rises to a lighting gantry of plain-sliced ash. Just beyond the fridge is what looks like a round floor-to-ceiling column. It isn't. Covered in a zebra-wood veneer, it contains six lazy-Susan shelves tucked discreetly behind two curved doors. "It's the best use of that corner we could possibly have," Hackett claimed.

Color plays a major role in the success of the new kitchen. What Hackett described as "an earthy plum tone" on some base cabinets extends to the 18-by-18-inch terrazzo floor tiles and 1-inch-square glass mosaic wall tiles, which repeat that color along with orange plus the light and medium browns of the various woods. Yellow-green paint on the wall framing the breakfast bar is the room's single splash of brilliant color.

Bausch recalled that her kitchen, as well as the rest of the house, was under renovation for a year and a half, but she insisted that the results were worth the work and the wait: "I knew I'd feel better in a new environment, and I was right. My kids are happier. So is my husband."

material matters

In the design of this small kitchen, function and finish materials frequently mesh in a useful tandem arrangement. A palette of six different woods plus tile, stone, and steel creatively delineates specific places and purposes throughout the room.

appliance garage A walnut tambour door rolls up to reveal a plugged-in coffee maker and toaster (top, left). Shelves above store cups and saucers for coffee and glasses for smoothies.

peninsula sink A drop-in mesh drain board (above, left) makes rinsing veggies a breeze; the raised lip on the custom concrete counter contains drips.

pull-out base Condiment storage on two tiers (above, left) is placed behind a plain-sliced figured ash cabinet face.

corner tower Curved doors of zebra-wood veneer hide six lazy-Susan shelves (above). The lower ones store packaged foods; the two near counter height hold everyday dishware; the top is for snacks.

spice cupboard Mounted on the stainless steel wall beside the cooktop (below, left) is a cabinet with a touch-latch door. The door front is a collage of Macassar ebony, walnut, and ash woods.

toekick storage Between the wall oven and the floor is a 4-inch-deep walnut-fronted drawer (below) for trays, cookie sheets, and a cupcake pan.

Between microwave and oven is a pull-out butcher-block shelf for items removed from either appliance. Above the microwave are cabinets with dividers for vertical plate storage.

one size befitting all

the biggest challenge in most kitchen renovations is coaxing a small space to live and work large. John and Sue Wieland confronted the opposite scenario when they set out to update the design-challenged kitchen in their two-story 1933 Colonial in suburban Atlanta.

Once they had removed the wall separating the vintage pantry from the principal food-prep space in the kitchen, a very spacious U-shaped area was revealed. Then, in collaboration with Atlanta-based designer Matthew D. Rao, CKD, they devised an inviting floor plan that put all of the room's 580 square feet to good use.

A key theme of the design strategy was doubling up: The kitchen has two wine coolers, two sinks, two 27-inch ovens, and a 6-foot-wide side-by-side commercial refrigerator/freezer that looks like two matching units. The focal point of this contemporary classic design, where traditional-style cabinetry in white oak is paired with sleek stainless steel hardware, is the 10½-foot-long, L-shaped central island, which houses a six-burner cooktop, a built-in steamer, a deep sink especially for caterers, and a breakfast bar and stools. "We used four levels and four different surface materials—butcher block, honed black granite, stainless steel, and crystal-clear Starfire glass—to break things up," Rao declared. "Because of this, the island doesn't look as big as it really is; yet at parties there is lots of room for the caterers to work and for guests to mingle."

The idea of pairs is carried through to the cabinetry. The steel-fronted appliance garages over the ovens, for example, are arranged in twos to evoke the feeling of an old-fashioned larder. "I chose to work with two-foot modules," said Rao. "They create a comfortable scale and rhythm in the space. And I played with the dimensions of the cabinetry's recessed panels, making their frames wider to create interesting, more contemporary patterns."

The Wielands reported that because of the close attention being paid to the myriad design details, the kitchen, despite its size, quickly became the heart of the home. "I entertain a lot during the day—my book club meets here often," Sue reported. "Everybody likes to have parties at our house so they can hang out in the kitchen." That, John said, can be a small problem: "Nobody wants to go to any other room."

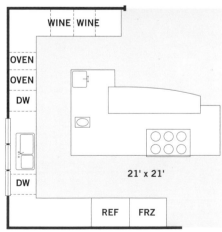

ABOVE: Once merged with an old butler's pantry, the kitchen faced the rare challenge of being much too big. One way designer Matthew Rao brought it back into scale visually was by retaining the room's varying ceiling heights.

RIGHT: A six-burner cooktop is flanked by different counter surface materials. Their variety lessens the massive impact of the island, which is more than 10 feet long.

ultra-big basin A graphic element in its own right, the deep sink (above) is made of honed black granite. It easily conceals the oversize pots and pans used mainly by caterers at parties.

hidden assets In this kitchen, all the base cabinets are white oak. Rather than interrupt this look, the stainless steel dishwasher door has been clad in a matching wood panel (right).

veggie heaven Particularly for a family that likes their greens hot and healthy, the supreme convenience of a built-in countertop steamer (below, right) simply shouldn't be underestimated.

sharp thinking As any cook will attest, knives quickly lose their edges when stored in a jumble in drawers. A custom cutlery block (below) protects blades—and fingers—from nicks.

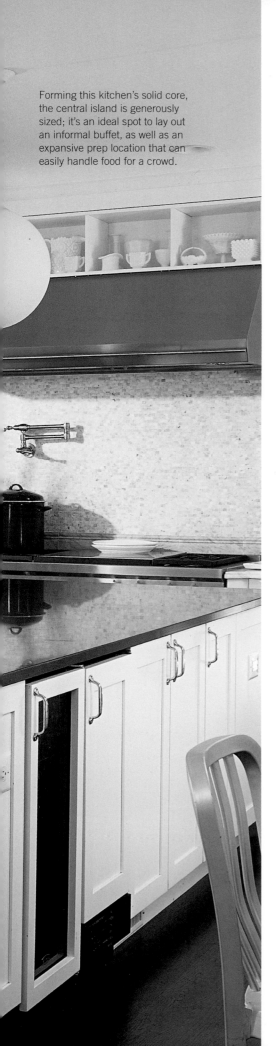

double or nothing

chalk it up to growing pains.
When interior designer Kiki Luthringshausen learned she was pregnant with her fourth child, she and husband Vincent Florack faced an important decision: Should they stay put and remodel their 10-year-old home, or flee the familiar west-Chicago suburb and buy a larger house somewhere else?

Rather than uproot the family, the couple finally opted to remodel—with Kiki at the helm. "I was ready for my dream kitchen," recalled the designer, a self-described foodie and talented cook, whose skill and creativity routinely dazzle family and friends. Although she admits there was nothing seriously wrong with the 440-square-foot space, her expanding family (and growing guest list) cried out for additional space for prep and storage, plus a larger dining area. "After doing other people's kitchens for the past 11 years, it was time to do mine," she added.

Inspired by the straightforward style that characterizes 19th-century service kitchens, she created a symmetrical, U-shaped floor plan anchored by two islands. She then borrowed freely from the past, adopting a classic black-and-white palette, fitted floor-to-ceiling cabinets, no-nonsense stainless

steel fixtures, and ebony-stained hardwood floors. "I loved the look but wanted to make it my own," she said, explaining her decision to pair luxe materials—thick slabs of white Calcutta marble and ebony granite—with simple commercial appliances and fixtures like her favorite faucet, a practical prerinse model employed by restaurant kitchens. Eclectic decorative elements, including a pair of kitschy globe lights that illuminate the main island, also factored into the mix.

Standard appliances were exchanged for pro-style versions, including a 60-inch range equipped with a double griddle, which traditionally sees action each Saturday when pancakes top the menu. "The kids love it," said Kiki, who enjoys cooking for her children and their pals on weekends. "No one ever leaves our table hungry."

Her kitchen's two islands create a pair of granite-topped work areas. The main island handles prep and entertaining chores and is more than two and a half times larger than the original. A second, peripheral unit provides pull-up seating for casual meals. Equipped with a small fridge stocked with juice boxes and fruit, it allows easy access to snacks while

living large

Convenience and cosmetics share equal billing here. No kitchen can rely strictly on the luxury of size to hide any design flaws. Here is how polish meets performance in this busy family kitchen.

a beauty of a breakfront Tall cabinet doors fronted with panels of ribbed glass let color and silhouettes show through (left). The cupboards nearest the ceiling have lighted interiors, the better to highlight a collection of milk glass that originally belonged to the homeowner's grandmother.

hot topic The microwave often poses a paradox in the kitchen: It is frequently used, so it must be readily accessible, but generally it's not aesthetically worthy of prominent display. Recessing the appliance into an open shelf deftly addresses both issues (below, left).

fill 'er up Running a cold-water line up through the wall behind the range permitted the installation of a pot filler at the point of usage (above, right). A slight modification of a commercial design, it has shut-off valves at both the wall and the end of the spigot. It is also jointed, so it can fold out of the way.

thinking twice Whenever practical, designer Kiki Luthringshausen doubled up on appliances, explaining that with a large family, "two dishwashers make everything so much easier." Her drawer-style units (right) were positioned so they can be loaded easily by the children.

keeping the kids far out of the kitchen's principal work zone.

Thanks to meticulously planned storage, counters remain free and clear. Each cabinet and drawer is content-specific right down to the large dish cupboard positioned low so the children can easily retrieve plates, cups, and cutlery. A super-size lazy Susan stows small appliances.

With the family-friendly space completed, Kiki planned to take on other home projects. What's up next? "The rest of house," she confided. "Our kitchen is finished now, but I still don't want anyone to go upstairs!"

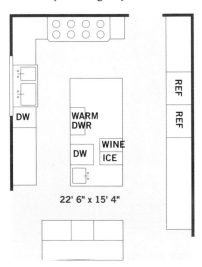

ABOVE: Appliances are arranged on both sides of the island as well as around the kitchen perimeter. The island's scale and content make it an appropriate as well as convenient place for all of the family meal-making chores.

open-plan design

Remove walls, create flow-through spaces—these are earmarks of the typical open-plan remodel. In kitchen design, it means merging cooking and dining, or cooking and family living. Often it means creating a great room—the kitchen, living and dining rooms all in one big space. For critics it signals loss of privacy for the family cook, but for adherents it means the end of isolation for anyone preparing meals or serving drinks and food. Open-plan design reflects a specific lifestyle that, for some, may suggest a radical change.

learning his living

OPPOSITE: In redoing his own kitchen, designer Timothy Huber hunted for bargains and waited for the right deal. The laminate floor, for example, came from a store that was just about to shut down.

seasoned design pros have redone so many tired, old kitchens that it would be logical to suppose the process would be old hat. Somehow, though, when it comes to their own kitchens—where they should be the ultimate hands-on visionaries—even designers can learn a few things. Actually, make that a lot of things.

Not long ago, Phoenix-area designer Timothy Huber bought a 1,200-square-foot tract house built in the mid-1950s. At the time, he had been a certified kitchen designer for two years and had worked at a custom cabinet shop for seven years before that. He had extensive experience in design but little in actual construction. So buying his own home gave him an opportunity for on-site learning.

In no hurry and determined to cut costs wherever possible, Huber took on the entire renovation himself, though he handed over some electrical and plumbing work to other pros. "I was familiar with how things worked, so I just did it," he said, "and I learned more about the whole process along the way." He had his work cut out for him.

So determined was he to breathe freshness into the dreary home, he had drawn up blueprints for a full-gut renovation before he had even closed on the house. The core of his plan was to open up the typically cramped layout of the home by tearing down three load-bearing walls. (The new structural members are concealed in the ceiling, Huber explained.) With the floor plan upgraded, he focused on the kitchen, filling that space with such amenities as stainless steel appliances, natural-finished maple cabinets, and faux-wood laminate on the floor and backsplash.

"The house had the original baths, the original fuse box, no dishwasher; there wasn't even a vent fan in the kitchen," he recalled. Five years—and many working weekends—later, Huber had transformed the worn, dated house into a bright, open, contemporary-style home with every modern convenience.

To save money, Huber took his time throughout the construction process, waiting for materials he wanted at prices he could afford. The laminate flooring came from a store that was going out of business, for example, and a friend built the glass dividing walls in the living room for barter. Solid-surfacing counters that resemble terrazzo look more upscale than they really are, and Huber assembled the cabinets himself to reduce labor costs.

Even the eye-catching backsplash behind the cooktop was a bargain, created from leftover scraps of laminate flooring.

Thoughtful design details throughout distinguish the kitchen. A curved, dropped-ceiling treatment above the dining area, for example, provides visual interest and defines the eating space without sealing it off from the rest of the room.

When the job was completed, Huber insisted that years of hands-on labor were well worth the effort. "Because I did the work myself, I was able to put more detail into the house than I would have otherwise. I never could have paid somebody to do all that work," he said.

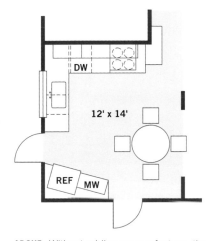

ABOVE: Without adding square footage, the designer created a compact plan that included essential appliances and work surfaces and also made room for a stylish kitchen table and chairs.

TOP: With terrazzo countertops so costly, Huber chose solid surfacing to replicate that very look for less. He used leftover laminate flooring to create an attractive, though frugal, backsplash.

ABOVE: Base cabinets where the cooktop and oven stand were bumped out 6 inches, adding drawer and work space. That "drawer" above these appliances is a pull-out ventilation unit.

sizing up a room

Faced with a small kitchen, designer Timothy Huber took several measures to ensure the room would both look and function like a much larger space. First, he removed three load-bearing walls between the kitchen and the family room. Even though the footprint was unchanged, the now wide-open kitchen gives the illusion of being larger than it is. Next, he increased the depth of base cabinets on the cooking wall from 24 to 30 inches, adding a countertop surface. Finally, a well-planned cabinet arrangement made the most of both storage and work space. A clever cabinet door to the left of the refrigerator and just beneath the microwave, for instance, can be pulled down and locked into place. It's a hideaway countertop that can be stashed out of sight when not in use. And a custom-designed pull-out cabinet to the right of the oven is actually a spice rack.

RIGHT: Below the microwave is a pull-down door that hides small appliances. In a pinch, that door can become an extra shelf—or a landing place for foods as they are removed from the refrigerator.

FAR RIGHT: A grid partition separates the living room from other parts of the house. The lattice is solid maple, and the panels are polycarbonate. The open shelves and end panels adjacent to the grid are maple veneer.

BELOW: Removing three load-bearing walls opened up the space so that the kitchen and family room could flow together completely, becoming a single uninterrupted space.

harnessing height

"the house is an Edwardian, not a Victorian," Rob Cox insisted. "It was built in 1901." What he and his wife, Suzanne Cutts, bought in 1997 was a three-story San Francisco residence near a neighborhood of other restored "painted ladies."

According to Cutts, "There was still a lot of the original detail, all of which we've tried to retain." Their biggest challenge was the kitchen, located on the second floor. It had been redone on the cheap in the late 1970s, and the space was not used well. Also, its white-painted cabinets were pressboard, and there was a brick chimney rising up from the furnace that took a whole corner out of the room.

When the couple concluded they could no longer function in that kitchen, they sought out Tim Wong, of Buttrick Wong Architects in Emeryville, California. "We'd seen his firm's work in a magazine," Cutts recalled. "The story showed space being utilized in such a way that I knew these were the people who could help us. We wanted change but weren't going to alter our kitchen's footprint."

"We could have," Cox added, "except that there is a 100-year-old bougainvillea just outside the kitchen.

It's a tree, not a vine, and its canopy crowns our deck with fuchsia-colored flowers. Tim knew he'd be working within a very narrow, defined space."

The five-month remodel began in earnest when the kitchen was gutted. "Everything was rearranged," Wong recalled. "We ripped out two narrow walls that had been put up on either side of the old range, added an island that was nearly seven feet long and replaced the existing flush window with a bay window and window seat." The slight protrusion of the window setup added only 18 inches of space but definitely made the room feel bigger.

In addition to the spatial shuffle, Wong replaced outmoded surfaces. Gone was the linoleum floor. In its place was new white-oak flooring stained to match oak floors in the rest of the house, all of which had been refinished. Banished, too, was the space-gobbling chimney. It became obsolete when a new furnace and water heater were installed. The new refrigerator is approximately where the old one stood, but removing the brick stack made it possible to build in that appliance, add storage cabinets above it, and put a pull-out, adjustable-shelf pantry beside it. (The new furnace is

serviced by a narrow tubular chimney enclosed neatly within the wall.)

Finally, the kitchen was configured to flow more smoothly into the dining room by removing the old swinging door and widening the opening. It is now six feet across and includes a pair of wood-framed glass pocket doors that can be pulled shut when needed.

With the infrastructure taken care of, the architect turned to Cutts's personal requests. "I told Tim I needed a lot of counter space," she said. "I wanted a place that would be really comfortable for people hanging out while I'm cooking. The best thing in the world for me is the bookcase Tim designed—it's notched into the island. Also, because it's taller than the island, people can put their wine glasses or plates on it without getting in the way of my cooking." On the work side of the island there's a convection microwave plus storage drawers and a cabinet designed for trays and cookie sheets.

The result of all the work done is a space worth bragging about, whether the home is Edwardian or Victorian. "What we got was pretty much what we asked for," Cutts concluded. "There's nothing I would change. I absolutely love this kitchen."

RIGHT: The new kitchen occupies the same footprint as the old one, but architect Tim Wong reconfigured the space, taking out two narrow walls and a chimney. His more open plan also includes plentiful countertop work space, which the homeowners specifically requested.

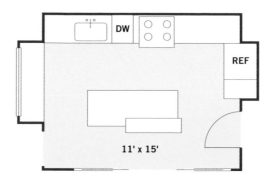

11' x 15'

OPPOSITE: One convenience that really delighted the family cook was the human energy–saving pot filler faucet installed conveniently over the range.

vertical access

With their kitchen's 13-foot ceiling height, the owners were able to extend everything upward without making the 11-by-15-foot space feel crowded.

found storage A slender slice of space next to the refrigerator (left) was not wasted. Instead, it was transformed into a tall pantry, providing front-to-back access to oils, condiments, and other cooking staples.

hook the ladder The solid construction and sturdy, reliable hardware of the sliding ladder (below) was central to the success of this remodel. The ladder's cherry stain and turned rungs help it fit in with the look of the space.

that filling feeling A fold-out faucet directly over the range (opposite) makes filling a tall pot for pasta or stock an easy task. The owners purchased the range when they first moved in; it became the only existing item in the kitchen that survived the remodeling.

BELOW: The ladder fulfilled an important accessibility function, allowing the storage and display of pieces high overhead. Directly below the foot-deep wall cabinets is open shelving, only 7 inches deep, that stores regularly needed items.

BELOW, RIGHT: Celadon ceramic subway tiles measuring 3 by 6 inches have a crackled finish. They add texture as well as beauty, and, explained Cutts, "you can run your hands on them and actually feel the bumps."

OPPOSITE: The new window is no bigger than the old one, but being a bay, it extends the room outward. It also adds seating and storage. Architect Wong made a niche for the ladder by carving out space in the window-seat area.

all-wood wonder

take one pair of doting grandparents. Add 18 grandchildren of toddler to college age, plus all their parents. Sprinkle in a wide variety of friends. Mix in a careful and versatile design, and you have the perfect recipe for a kitchen in a contemporary home in the Connecticut woods.

"This is a second home for the owners; they wanted a kitchen formal enough for large catered parties yet casual enough for the grandkids to come sit at the counter and grab a quick bite," according to architect Elizabeth Gray, of New Haven, Connecticut–based Gray Organschi Architecture, who designed the three-level house on the side of a hill. "It's like a sophisticated tree house."

The 300-square-foot, free-flowing kitchen is ideal for the style of entertaining the owners enjoy. One end

of the room sits on-grade, facilitating the easy transport of groceries from the car; the other end opens onto an elevated grassy courtyard and garden, where fresh herbs await picking. The space adjoins a formal living room dominated by a stone fireplace that's nearly big enough to stand in.

The kitchen's simple style, which includes birch plywood cabinets, Chinese limestone flooring, and cast-concrete countertops, was designed to emphasize the openness of the architecture. An illuminated glass backsplash adds more task lighting where it's needed. A wall of shimmering mosaic tiles in orange, sienna, and ochre forms a graphic backdrop for the cooktop, and a sliding birch door linked to this wall shields the kitchen from guests during dinner parties.

Several styles of storage space add visual interest to the room. On the exterior wall overlooking the woods and pond, base cabinets provide drawer storage with open shelves and glass-fronted cabinets on the wall above. "We used frosted glass because we didn't want items inside to have to be perfectly arranged," Gray explained. "This helps because it's a big kitchen, and we wanted it to be

clear where everything is stored. We also varied the size of storage drawers so the owners could better remember where things are put away."

The kitchen, which is stylish without looking conventional, really springs to life, Gray said, "when the fire is going, the children are playing, the guests are mingling in the living room, and the cook is at the sink working and looking out at the pond."

where everything has a place

- Cabinets provide open and closed-door storage so that frequently used items are ready to grab at a moment's notice, and seldom-used ones remain mostly out of sight.

- The size and shape of the cabinet drawers and doors vary, adding interest and making it easier to remember what is stored where.

- Decorative frosted-glass panels lighten the look of some cabinets and obscure contents to the extent that nothing has to be neatly stacked and precisely positioned.

- Double islands mean double the storage capacity.

Because the kitchen serves as both a cooking and a gathering area, it has two each of ovens, dishwashers, sinks, full-size refrigerators, and islands. A 12-foot-long peninsula adds work space and provides room for casual dining.

material interest

shelf service Simple, shapely dishware is a pleasure to look at when framed by fixed shelves of varying sizes. Frosted glass doors obscure less-than-perfectly arranged items (left).

put 'er there Custom-fitted drawers (below, left) are de rigueur in a kitchen that's expected to serve many people. To handle large family gatherings efficiently, everything—from teaspoons to roasting pans—can be stowed with precision.

do an end run For convenience, and to avoid foot-traffic snarls in the kitchen, some storage can be accessed from outside the kitchen. Open shelves at the end of cabinet runs (below) add storage and are also great space-stretchers.

recessed relief An alcove next to the double wall ovens (top right) can act as either a set-down area (one island is opposite the ovens) or a display niche.

extra texture On the side of the peninsula that faces the dining area, using a perforated wooden screen maintains the materials palette but adds unexpected visual interest (right).

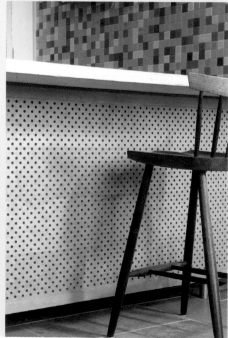

a space that flows

OPPOSITE: Guests seated at the dining table are spared the sight of drippy pans on the cooktop, thanks to a low backsplash on the island. Note the built-in steamer just to the left of the cooktop grates.

it's easy to imagine this urbane space crawling with glitterati and fashionistas. Indeed, its chic spareness and sophisticated fittings make it a glamorous backdrop. But, in truth, the room was originally designed with a different type of user in mind.

A couple with growing children live in this two-story contemporary Prairie-style house in Calgary, Alberta. Its 250-square-foot L-shaped kitchen was designed by the wife, who sited the kitchen at the back of the house and combined it with the living and dining rooms to create a large communal area. The end result is an open-plan interior that is easy on the eye and similarly easy for kids and adults to navigate—important qualities for a heavy-traffic household.

"We always have a steady stream of guests," she recalled. "Our four kids bring their friends home, and we often host their parents, too. This kitchen is like one big entertainment area with three spaces, and I designed it so our living room furniture can be brought into the kitchen whenever additional seating is needed."

To make sure that the cook is always the life of the party, the island's prep area and cooktop face toward the living room and its double-sided fireplace. For larger, fair-weather gatherings, French doors on a windowed wall swing open, beckoning guests to mingle on the covered patio. As the wife explained, "When we had a big make-your-own-pizza party, everyone moved around easily and comfortably, just flowing with the floor plan."

A second sink, tucked onto a side wall, is convenient for cleanup, and its secluded position helps keeps dirty dishes out of sight. A similar function is performed at the island, where shallow stainless steel walls wrap around the back and side of the lowered cooktop, shielding its contents from view.

The space between the refrigerator and the china closet, which stands behind the island, does double duty as a personal gallery. Here, display niches showcase artwork and craft pieces, while a stainless steel shelf becomes a pedestal for vases. A pair of rectangular lighting fixtures, whose sandblasted glass shades match the fronts of the storage cabinets, complete the vignette.

Because the kitchen is so connected to the public spaces of the house, it had to be decorated to complement all those areas. To harmonize with the living room's polished look, the refrigerator and the freezer drawers on the island are paneled in the same espresso-stained rift-cut oak as the cabinets. Underfoot, blond maple flooring ties these elements together.

In the end, the kitchen is a pleasure to use, whether it's under the hectic conditions of feeding a gaggle of kids during an afternoon playdate ("Sometimes I feel like a short-order cook," the mom confided) or hosting an evening soirée for grownups.

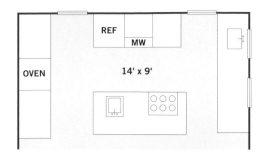

	REF	
	MW	
OVEN	14' x 9'	

LEFT: Walls came down and this kitchen opened up. Now, guests are free to eddy around the central island or gather in the adjoining dining and living areas.

BELOW: Low benches slide under the island's overhang when not in use, in keeping with a neat appearance and a chic atmosphere. Views of the living areas are also preserved—all the better for keeping an eye on the kids.

functional and suitable for all

Despite its sophisticated appearance, this kitchen was laid out as a family-friendly space. Having a household full of youngsters inspired several design decisions:

a good wood The cabinets are constructed of oak, a durable hardwood, and finished in a deep, dirt-disguising espresso tone.

counter point The kitchen island is topped with a quartz-based material that creates a hardy work surface. It doesn't stain and holds up well under many years of heavy use and abuse.

stain bane The benches that pull up to two sides of the island are upholstered in a microfiber fabric, which is washable.

hands off The stainless steel perimeter counters have a matte-finish surface pattern that is guaranteed to obscure every stray little hand- and fingerprint.

too high to handle Breakable items and seldom-used equipment are stored on the uppermost shelves, reachable only by climbing a rolling library ladder.

in perfect balance

a place for everything is what Mark and Patti Kogan knew they wanted, as they have always had their kitchen routine down pat: He does most of the cooking for the family, and she does most of the cleanup. So when they remodeled their Orinda, California, home they created a kitchen that "worked" for both of them in all senses of the word.

Medium-gray oak cabinets and a 4-by-8-foot stainless steel island, both from Arclinea San Francisco, the kitchen cabinet and design firm that executed the new space, bring elegance and beauty to the 14-by-16-foot room. The kitchen's sleek interior houses a host of organizers that allow Patti, a certified public accountant, to store everything from oversize stock pots to paring knives.

"Everything is easily accessible and close to where we do the work," said Mark, a physician. "The silverware drawer is right next to the dishwasher, for example." Eriche Wilson, owner of Arclinea San Francisco, readily concurred, as such convenience was, from the beginning, part of the plan.

Two tall vertical storage units, with drawers on the bottom and doors on top, and a pullout pantry filled with wire baskets anchor the refrigerator and wine cooler. A counter-to-ceiling appliance garage near the double ovens conveniently consolidates the collection of small appliances—microwave, coffeemaker, toaster, and blender. Its retractable shelf is sized right to hold a dinner plate and coffee cup.

On either side of the cooktop is a 6-inch-wide pull-out base cabinet. This handy tandem holds essential products, most notably oils and vinegars. "Patti likes to keep things in order and to have everything immaculate," Wilson explained, "so we chose stainless steel for the backsplash because it is easy to clean. The cabinets don't have hardware for the same reason. The result is understated elegance that's also highly functional. It's a kitchen made to be cooked in."

Often, at mealtimes, one or the other of the Kogans' two teenage children pitch in. At such times, having a pair of sinks makes it easy for two people

RIGHT: Gray cabinets come to life thanks to tasteful, vibrant accents and a carefully thought-out lighting plan. "The stainless steel island reflects light, making the space much brighter," according to designer Eriche Wilson.

BELOW: Ramping up storage and carefully mapping it out were equally important to making this remodel a success. "We doubled the efficiency of our kitchen without adding any square feet," said homeowner Mark Kogan.

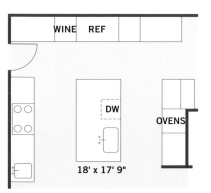

WINE REF

DW

OVENS

18' x 17' 9"

LEFT: What's the key to making this flexible floor plan work like a charm? Actually, it's the two sinks. The primary basin serves the dishwasher; the secondary sink, near the cooktop, saves the chef from doing end-runs around the island.

to be working at once. The main sink is on the island, and a food-prep basin is near the cooktop. Setting the table is a snap because glassware and dishes are kept in glass-fronted cabinets close to the dining area of the kitchen.

Even the desk does kitchen duty: It's conveniently placed in a quiet corner, and the shelves mounted directly above it are packed with cookbooks, making it an ideal place for Mark to research new recipes.

what's in storage

Hardware manufacturers have created many ways of making and using drawers and cabinets. Thanks to the skillful engineering of hinges, drawer slides, and interior organizers, a cabinet can now have no hardware on the outside but be filled with practical amenities inside.

tune into the channel In lieu of a knob or pull, a channel running along the side of a cabinet or the top of a drawer (above) serves as a handle. This leaves the front unadorned—and really easy to clean.

smooth running Don't even worry about that channel groove being difficult to grip. Current hinges and drawer slides have been cleverly designed for easy opening and soft closing.

organize it Taking a cue from the Dutch artist Piet Mondrian, European hardware makers conceived a modular drawer system (above) that uses dividers and metal trays to create organizational harmony among the bottle stoppers, lemon reamers, balls of butcher's twine, and miscellaneous gadgets that tend to migrate to the deep, forgotten recesses of the utensil drawer. (Note how the drawer pulls out all the way for total access.)

high on convenience When choosing tall pantries, you have several options: You can install a series of roll-out shelves and mount a rack on the inside door surface. Or opt for pull-outs accessible from both sides. Here, storage drawers and pantries (right and opposite) are paired in two cabinet units. As you can see, variations are practically limitless.

organizing aids

There are many plausible ways to de-clutter your kitchen effectively without making it impossible to locate and access the items you use most often. Consider these possibilities:

■ **use every nook** Never underestimate the effectiveness of harnessing small, underutilized areas in your kitchen. Example: A narrow space beside your wall oven or refrigerator can become storage space for brooms, sweepers, and dustpans organized in a tall cabinet. Keeping these items tucked away, rather than left out, will make your kitchen less cluttered and your kitchen life more enjoyable.

■ **add extra display spaces** Build shelving or niches between the ceiling and the top of a row of wall cabinets, an often-overlooked area that can become a dynamic focal point. Another possibility: A slightly raised shelf at the back of the counter is potentially good use of space, as it provides storage without actually encroaching on the countertop.

■ **make room for spices** Keep spice jars, bottles, and tins handy but off your countertops by storing them upright in a drawer. Check out the variety of in-drawer storage systems available at housewares stores and home centers. It's important to make sure that each container you use has its own identifiable slot, so you can always locate what you need.

■ **open up shelving** Stack dishes and bowls neatly on easily accessed open, horizontal shelves, and store large plates in an open, vertical shelf unit. Baking sheets can be stored vertically or horizontally, depending on available shelf height and width. Ready-made racks for vertical plate storage can be wall-mounted or tucked in a corner of your counter, always within reach.

■ **sneak drawers in** A set of drawers or freestanding drawer units tucked under an existing bench will provide storage space for everything from place mats and table linens to holiday decorations.

■ **put vegetables on display** Wicker baskets on open shelves are ideal receptacles for fresh vegetables awaiting use rather than destined for the refrigerator. Most long, narrow, shelf-size baskets can hold up to seven pounds of produce, which can actually "breathe" better when stored this way.

■ **revive dead space** That shallow space directly under your kitchen sink need not go to waste. Consider tucking in a freestanding base cabinet with a tilt-out drawer—to hold sponges and brushes that might otherwise get lost in the perennial kitchen shuffle.

■ **borrow designer details** Unless there is a closed cabinet under your sink, keeping the area neat and well organized can be challenging. Hanging a mini curtain on a spring-rod across the opening will add visual interest to that part of your kitchen and also shield from view a variety of items you may want to keep unseen.

mini storage miracles

Here's how to maximize the storage space you have and make more room for all of your gear. Scan your kitchen with some of these tips in mind:

■ Install sliding or rolling shelves to create easier access to items stored in the back of deep cabinets.

■ Harness the heights: Use a library ladder on runners to reach cabinet tops or the top row of floor-to-ceiling storage units.

■ Make it possible to store trays or flat pans in the open space between the refrigerator and overhead cabinetry.

■ Ease crowding in cupboards by moving most-used cookware to hooks on a hanging wrought-iron pot rack.

■ Transform toe-kick space beneath a wall oven into a drawer for cookie tins and baking dishes, or a flat niche for a folding stepstool.

■ Tier canned goods on a multi-shelved rack to make them more visible and accessible.

■ Bring kitchen dead space to life with corner shelf units.

■ Add casters so freestanding storage or shelf units can be moved around where needed.

■ Add a compact rolling island complete with drawers, shelves, and usable work surfaces.

■ Make or buy X-shaped inserts to turn storage cubes into holders for wine, water, or soda bottles.

■ Hang dish towels and oven mitts from glass knobs screwed to the end of a base cabinet. Or mount a swing-out towel rack near the sink.

■ If you have room, build a bench or window seat with drawers underneath for storing oversize and seldom-used items.

■ Arrange everyday condiments on an attractive turntable.

■ Hang a tidy grocery-bag holder on the inside of a door.

■ Show off heirloom china on tiered plate racks; save closed-cabinet space for everyday dishes.

■ Retrofit oversize kitchen drawers with a layered set of sliding shelves for cookware. Or put dividers in deep drawers so each pot has a place.

■ Liberate cabinet or drawer space by storing spices on a shelf or in a wall rack near your range or cooktop. Or attach a heavy-duty rail system along your backsplash and mount a rack on it to hold essential spices.

■ To create a convenient place to store kitchen knives, attach a magnetic strip to the wall near your cooktop, range, or meal-prep area .

■ Maximize drawer space: Use cutlery dividers to organize knives, forks, and spoons. Or keep everyday tableware in a silverware caddy right on the counter.

■ Add a shelf near your meal-prep area for cooking oils, or near the sink for cleaning products.

- Hang shallow racks for pot-lid holders or mitt hooks in what is usually wasted space on the inside of wall-cabinet doors.

- Install pull-out racks under the sink to hold containers for trash, recycled materials, or cleaning products.

- Arrange to dispense soda cans from special holders made for refrigerators or cabinets.

- Display attractive, colorful, but seldom-used serving pieces—platters and large bowls—along the tops of wall cabinets, rather than inside.

- Store spatulas and other frequently used utensils in stainless steel or ceramic canisters placed as close as possible to your cooking surface.

- Conserve some of your precious counter and shelf space by storing fresh fruits or vegetables in ceiling-hung tiered wire baskets.

- Add under-shelf racks within wall cabinets to expand cupboard space.

- Build shelving at one end of a kitchen island for cookbooks.

- Find room for a pantry cabinet. A tall, narrow one with pull-out shelves could go next to a freestanding refrigerator, adding needed storage space plus a built-in look.

- Create shelf space in your dining room's china cabinet so you can move everyday dishes and tableware out of the kitchen.

- Don't waste space in corner base cabinets; install lazy Susans so that stored items are never pushed too far back to be seen or used.

- Look for hidden storage spaces: With a stud finder, locate studs in your kitchen wall. Knock out the drywall between them and build shelves or create niches there.

fit for a pro

Truly professional kitchens are designed for commercial use—by restaurant chefs and caterers. Cooking appliances produced for them tend to be heavy and hot, so floors must be structured to provide needed support; heat barriers must be installed between ranges and flanking cabinets; and ventilation must be powerful enough to capture and remove all of the smoke, steam, and heat produced in the space.

Because of the attraction such appliances created, starting back in the 1980s, many manufacturers began producing appliances that resembled what pros were trained to use. That attraction persists, as strong as ever.

Yes, pro-style units do include extra features and amenities unknown to home cooks in earlier times: for example, ultra high-heat burners, low-heat simmer burners, and exhaust hoods that express the ultimate in cutting-edge design. But these are mainly modifications. Keep in mind that, in most instances, professional style is mainly that—a look. Gifted home cooks can always whip up superlative meals and dishes on more modest equipment. And the truth is, you don't need a professional-style kitchen just to feed your family or entertain friends.

However, having a well-organized, handsomely equipped space can ensure that yours is an inviting haven for all who work or gather there. Here's how to make your kitchen cook-friendly:

■ Create a dedicated baking area by outfitting a section of countertop with a long marble slab.

■ Replace a standard kitchen faucet with a high gooseneck model to make filling deep pots easier.

■ Substitute glass inserts for wood panels in key wall-cabinet doors to show off collectibles or attractive dishes and glassware.

■ Add to your display options: Install glass shelves high within the framework of a kitchen window so that your stored glassware will sparkle in the moon- or sunlight.

■ Outfit the sink with a customized cutting board so vegetable peelings and waste can be swept into the drain or disposer easily.

■ Consider installing a second sink strictly for cleanup.

■ Find room for an undercounter-model wine cooler—preferably in a bar area, a peninsula, or an island.

■ To keep kitchen knives handy, attach a magnetic bar to the wall nearest your food-prep area.

■ Install storage grids along one wall to hold pot lids and miscellaneous kitchen gear.

■ Create an appliance garage so often-used small appliances—your mixer, toaster, food processor, and coffeemaker—are kept out of sight without being totally out of reach.

■ Keep grains, rice, pasta, and beans in transparent glass or plastic containers for textural interest as well as storage practicality. They can dress up your counter, and you will always know when to restock.

■ Fit that often overlooked empty space above the refrigerator with a cabinet containing vertical dividers designed to hold trays.

- Illuminate counters and work areas with subtle under-cabinet lights: energy-saving fluorescent tubes or a measured strand of halogen bulbs.

- To record shopping needs, hang a small, nicely framed chalkboard on the wall, or have a chalkboard panel inserted into a wall-cabinet door.

- To vary the level of ambient lighting in your kitchen, replace the on/off switches with dimmers.

- To create a special place for snacking or enjoying light meals, attach a hinged half-circle surface to one end of a base cabinet.

- Create undercounter shelf space for your microwave and toaster oven so that kids can access them easily.

- Consider acquiring an undercounter beverage center so you can move sodas and juices out of your fridge.

- Space permitting, add shelves to hold most-used cookbooks.

- Mount a pull-down cookbook holder on the underside of a wall cabinet.

easy kitchen upgrades

Even the simplest alterations can add new life and appeal to your kitchen without incurring the cost or hassle of a major remodel. New paint, wallpaper, trim, tiles, chair cushions, valances, floor runners, coordinated table linens, and other decorating efforts can provide instant renewal of a tired space. Here are other suggestions:

- Transform wall cabinets with clear-glass insert door panels. Or install panels of translucent frosted glass to create a feeling of openness without having to put all of your cabinet contents on direct display.

- Put up molding to give the kitchen greater architectural interest.

- Apply molding strips to create the illusion of paneling on flat-surface cabinet doors. Add paint or stain for a complete freshening.

- Remove some cabinet doors and create open shelves for displaying pretty pottery or serving ware.

- Install small lights inside glass-fronted cabinets to show off your collectibles more dramatically.

- Using favorite tiles or textiles as inspiration, paint a measured stack of unglazed tiles, then have them fired at a DIY ceramic center and applied as a decorative backsplash.

- Cover a worn, unattractive floor with new self-adhering vinyl tiles. Or fashion a floorcloth by cutting a piece of oilcloth to fit the worn floor area near your sink. Paint to pick up colors or patterns in your window treatments or favorite china. For durability, polyurethane your work.

- Spruce up wood cabinet surfaces by stripping them and applying a finish that's either lighter or darker than the current one.

- Paint cabinet interiors a contrasting color for optimal impact.

- Redo window treatments in luscious colors, a chore that can be as easy as clipping the points of linen napkins to a curtain rod.

- Turn an unused wood table into an island. To add a useful work surface, top the island with butcher block or a marble or granite slab.

- Replace cabinet hardware. Porcelain knobs, figurative handles, or vintage-style metal pulls can add new life and a coordinated look to any-age cabinetry.·

- Update the look and efficiency of your kitchen sink with a stylish new faucet set.

- Mount a single open shelf under wall cabinets to hold mugs, cereal bowls, and other everyday dishes.

- Install pegboard panels on empty walls. Paint in jaunty colors, then after positioning the hooks, paint "shadow" outlines so that every item hung there can be returned to its proper place after use.

- Use letter transfers to spell out favorite foods or record a traditional family recipe on a kitchen wall.

- Paint the seats of wooden stools in colors that match your kitchen's wallpaper or wall tone.

- Install glass shelves in front of windows to hold cups, mugs, and pretty glass objects.

renewing your non-wood cabinet doors

It may seem daunting, but changing the look of veneered particleboard cabinetry is relatively simple if you follow these steps:

1. Clean surfaces with an all-purpose cleaner or an oxycleaner formulated to remove the accumulated dirt and grease.

2. Use a soft cloth or sponge dipped in clean, warm water to rinse off any cleaner residue.

3. Apply a stain-killing primer, which will bond to the veneer and create a good surface to paint on.

4. Let the primer dry for at least an hour, then brush on a coat of latex semigloss paint.

5. Allow the first coat of paint to dry overnight before smoothly applying a second coat.

The key to painting cabinets is to use a really good China-bristle paintbrush that holds a lot of paint. Note the following:

- A 2½-inch angled trim brush would work well here.

- Latex-based paint is recommended because it goes on so easily.

- Semigloss paint has a slight sheen that makes it comparatively easy to keep surfaces clean.

- Attach a painted wooden semicircle or rectangle to the wall with braced hinges. Pulled down, it will be a great place to have snacks or to utilize as a bonus serving surface; pushed up, it will virtually disappear.

- Create a new use for everyday objects. For example, drilling a hole in the base of a colorful enameled-metal colander can turn it into a pendant light shade.

- Add textural interest by exposing a brick wall or wood beams.

- Recycle aged wooden wine crates to use as shelf storage and also add country flair to your kitchen.

- Customize a standard unfinished armoire with bright paint to create a kitchen focal point with old-world charm and up-to-date storage.

- Make room for a small television so you can keep up with celebrity-chef shows on cable TV.

- Set aside space for a rocking chair or a comfortable lounge chair for relaxed recipe reading.

ventilation style

No matter what kind of cooking appliance you use, preparing meals inevitably heats up your kitchen and produces grease, smoke, and steam. These cooking byproducts can cloud the air in a kitchen and also accumulate on its surfaces, creating a dingy look. In addition, heat and steam can make the space unpleasant to work in and can ultimately damage your cabinet finish and tarnish your paint job. The solution: a properly ducted ventilation system sized to service all of the burners on your cooktop or range.

THREE FOR ALL

Ventilation systems comprise three wholly different categories: updraft, downdraft, and recirculating.

updraft systems installed directly over the cooking surface require a hood to collect vapors and, with help from a blower, push them through a series of ducts before funneling them to the outside. As hot air, smoke, and steam rise naturally, updraft units are considered the most efficient.

downdraft systems are either installed behind the cooking surface or integrated into the cooktop or range itself, using a fan to draw cooking vapors horizontally across the burners. Smoke and steam are evacuated through an exhaust duct. Caution: Due to their design, downdraft units lose effectiveness when you cook with very tall pots and pans. To work properly, a downdraft unit should rise 10 inches above cooktop level.

recirculating, or ductless, systems capture rising smoke and steam, which pass through a filter before being pumped back into the room. Often built into an over-the-range microwave, a recirculating unit can rid a room of most cooking odors. As it lacks the ability to remove heat or steam, however, it is not recommended for any heavy-use kitchen.

CLEARING THE AIR

The effectiveness of kitchen ventilation equipment is measured by the volume of air a system can move during the span of one minute. This number, a cubic-feet-per-minute reading (CFM), ranges from 100 to 1,800. The higher that number, the louder and more powerful the unit. The output capacity (Btus) and size of your cooking surface will dictate the correct hood size.

The National Kitchen & Bath Association (NKBA) recommends the following: 150 CFM for a unit installed over a basic gas or electric cooktop or range, and 600 CFM for a unit installed over a professional-style gas cooktop or range. Note that professional-style appliances with built-in grills and griddles often require ratings around 1,800 CFM.

FINDING THE BEST FIT

For peak performance, all ventilation units should be at least the same width as the cooking surface, but bigger is certainly better. Some experts suggest that the ideal model should be three or more inches wider, on either side, than the cooking surface.

According to NKBA guidelines, a hood that is 16 or 17 inches deep should be mounted 21 inches from the cooking surface; one that is 18 to 21 inches deep should be 24 inches from the surface; a 24-inch-deep hood should be mounted 30 inches above the surface. Note that if you choose an updraft rather than a recirculating system, you should give serious consideration to exactly how far the unit will extend out from the wall (to avoid the risk of bumping your head as you cook).

FEATURES AND FINISHES

Once you have settled on a particular style of ventilation equipment, consider the available features.

In addition to the basic designs that mainly move air, you will find ventilation units with built-in sensors that can monitor cooking activity and immediately switch the blower to a high setting when heat rising from the cooking surface reaches a level that is considered unacceptable.

There are also delayed turn-off features, which keep the blower running after the range or cooktop is turned off, and warming lights so that food is kept at the proper serving temperature.

Despite the ongoing popularity of decorative hood surrounds, edgier stainless steel designs have grown in appeal, particularly among those homeowners who want the cooking area to be their kitchen's focal point. If you are not keen on cleaning, however, so-called designer hoods may not be right for you. Anything made of metal or glass will show spots, thus will require extra care—it will have to be wiped thoroughly and often.

access for everyone

People with all of their abilities intact tend to take their physical skills for granted, failing to anticipate the physical or sensory limits that age or infirmity might ultimately create.

Today, however, forward-looking manufacturers are adding functional, flexible features to product lines, making it possible for prudent homeowners to have kitchens that will serve them well now and also respond to their needs in the future. In many instances, adhering to the strictures of universal design can make a kitchen a timeless investment and also an easier place for everyone to work in.

for cabinets, open shelving has the edge on closed cupboards because its contents are always visible, thus easily accessed, and also because a person in a wheelchair or with limited skills will not have to struggle to open cabinet drawers or doors.

drawer-style appliances, which have become popular with people of every age, offer handy amenities for anyone confined to a wheelchair. With dishwashers manufactured in this style, both drawers are designed to be easily opened, filled, and shut. Similarly, someone in a wheelchair would find it easy to access the freezer drawer of a bottom-mount refrigerator-freezer as well as the lower shelves of the refrigerator itself. Side-by-side-style models also offer accessibility benefits.

installing a wall oven 30 to 40 inches off the floor and placing a cooktop so that an open area exists below it are both great for wheelchair users. Separating an oven from a cooking surface this way can make a kitchen more accommodating to all in the family and can be a notable design plus in a kitchen that is often utilized by more than one cook.

avoid control knobs in favor of touch controls, which are effortless for anyone to operate—particularly a person whose mobility is compromised. Touchpad appliances rank high among the technologically most sophisticated kitchen products, along with induction cooktops and programmable ovens. Note that some appliance makers are now producing units with Braille or raised-letter controls.

consider induction cooking a safe as well as quick way to prepare meals. As this cooktop's burners will heat up only when magnetically conductive cookware is placed on them, this is an ideal choice for a household whose principal cook has impaired vision.

levers to push, rather than handles to turn, will ease the chore of turning tap water on and off. The ultimate alternative to gripping and twisting a handle is the hands-free faucet, in which an electronic eye controls water flow and temperature change. Note that a gooseneck spout is a plus for anyone having to fill a tall soup or pasta pot.

photo credits

Cover: David Duncan Livingston.
Back cover: top Claudio Santini;
center Sam Gray; bottom David Duncan
Livingston. Page 2: Susan Gilmore;
pages 8-9: Sam Gray; pages 10-13:
Robin Stubbert; pages 14-19: Eric
Piasecki; pages 20-23: Sam Gray;
pages 24-27: J. Savage Gibson; pages
28-31: Ed Gohlich; pages 32-35: Claudio
Santini; pages 36-39: Ken Gutmaker;
pages 40-41: Tria Giovan; pages 42-45:
Susan Gilmore; pages 46-49: David
Duncan Livingston; pages 50-53:
Tria Giovan; pages 54-59: David
Duncan Livingston; pages 60-63: Ken
Gutmaker; pages 64-67: John Gould
Bessler; pages 68-69: Jim Yochum;
pages 70-73: Mark Samu; pages 74-77:
David Duncan Livingston; pages
78-83: Ken Gutmaker; pages 84-87:
Sam Gray; pages 88-91: Jim Yochum;
pages 92-97: Jim Christy; pages 98-
103: Matthew Millman; pages 104-109:
Jeff McNamara; pages 110-113: Bruce
Edward; pages 114-117: David Duncan
Livingston.